SO-BCA-867

YOUR PSYCHIC POWERS
 a beginner's guide

CRAIG HAMILTON-PARKER

Headway · Hodder & Stoughton

Acknowledgements

My thanks to my clairvoyant wife Jane for all her support, and to Mark Eslick and Victor Rigby for their suggestions and technical help.

By the same author

The Psychic Workbook (Vermilion)

A catalogue entry for this title is available from the British Library

ISBN 0 340 674172

First published 1996
Impression number 10 9 8   7 6   5 4   3 2
Year   1999 1998 1997

Copyright © 1996 Craig Hamilton-Parker

All rights reserved. No part of this publication may be reproduced or transmitted in any form or by any means, electronic or mechanical, including photocopy, recording, or any information storage and retrieval system, without permission in writing from the publisher or under licence from the Copyright Licensing Agency Limited. Further details of such licences (for reprographic reproduction) may be obtained from the Copyright Licensing Agency Limited, of 90 Tottenham Court Road, London, W1P 9HE.

Typeset by Transet Limited, Coventry, England.
Printed in Great Britain for Hodder & Stoughton Educational, a division of Hodder Headline plc, 338 Euston Road, London NW1 3BH by Cox and Wyman Limited, Reading, Berks.

CONTENTS

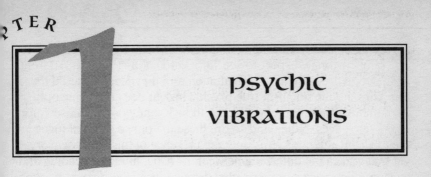

PSYCHIC VIBRATIONS

Have you had a psychic experience?

Turn to the personal column in the classified section of your local paper and you'll see a long list of advertisements from people offering their psychic services. Tarot, palmistry, numerology, tea-leaf reading – you name it and somebody's selling it. But do these practitioners have a true psychic gift? A person is not a medium, psychic or clairvoyant just because they say they are. In this book I will show you how to recognise true psychic powers and enhance them in yourself.

A psychic is someone who is sensitive to phenomena lying outside the range of normal experience. They may be able to see the future, communicate with the dead, see the aura, and be aware of vibrations beyond those normally perceived by the five senses. It is an ability that defies the laws of physics. It astonishes the open-minded and outrages sceptics. Yet psychic perception may be the next step in the evolution of human consciousness, one of nature's greatest gifts, currently rejected by society and exiled to the end of the pier. But the world is changing. People are looking for a meaning to this materialistic age. The old criteria no longer satisfy the urges of the soul. And you, as a reader of books like this, are probably one of the people who will help bring about this emerging change of perception.

A psychic has no need of the paraphernalia used by fortune-tellers. The public wrongly expect to see Tarot cards or a crystal ball in front of someone they pay for a consultation and they feel cheated if these trappings are missing. But true psychic insight does not come only from the interpretation of oracles. Although many psychics use Tarot cards, tea-leaves, palms and so on, these are only a point of focus for their psychic attention. It is only the presence of this super-sensory gift that makes the difference between a vague, muddled reading and a clear and precise one containing detailed facts about your situation that no one could possibly happen upon by guesswork.

Perhaps you've already had a paranormal experience of some kind, such as reading another's thoughts, seeing the auric light around living things or knowing who's on the end of the phone before you answer it. You may have travelled outside of your body, felt that you've lived through an event before, seen the dead or dreamed of the future. The psychic sense can be compared to a radio receiver that can be tuned to different frequencies. Most people are attuned to the five main sensory channels – sight, sound, touch, taste and smell, but turn the inner dial a little and you will become aware of other information: the vibration of thought, the flow of time, echoes from past lives, future conditions, energies radiating from living things, and the akashic blueprint that guides our destiny.

But before we launch ourselves into the fantastic let's take a sober look at how scientists have tried to categorise psychic and paranormal activities. What follows may not explain everything you have experienced but it clarifies our phraseology and may help you to identify the area in which your own experience falls.

ESP DEFINED

All psychic faculties come under the collective heading of Extra-Sensory Perception (ESP). This phrase was coined by the scientist Joseph B. Rhine, who headed a team of parapsychology investigators and devised experiments to gather empirical data to measure and

define these faculties. *ESP refers to any mental faculty which allows a person to acquire information about the world without the use of the known senses.* Rhine further clarified this by breaking ESP down into four main categories, dealt with in turn below.

Telepathy

We normally communicate with words, gestures and facial expression. However, Rhine proved that if all these sensory clues are eliminated and a person is placed in an isolated location and deliberately sent a specific target card, word or image by another person at another location, a communication can take place between one mind and another. The person receiving the thought 'sees' or 'senses' the target image. *Telepathy refers specifically to this transmission of information from one mind to another without the use of language, body movements, or any of the known senses.*

Clairvoyance

Clairvoyance literally means 'clear seeing' and has fallen into colloquial usage as another name for 'second sight'. Some people also misuse the word to mean seeing the future. However the meaning in parapsychology is quite specific. *Clairvoyance is the acquisition by a mind of information which is not available to it by the known senses and which is not known at the time to any other mind.* In other words, it is about picking up information that nobody knows and can't inadvertently send you by telepathy. For example, if the person can, excluding tricks of course, read the pages of a closed book or give the sequence of a shuffled pack of cards that have not been seen by anyone else – this is clairvoyance. (And just to confuse things further, mediums, who communicate with the dead, consider clairvoyance as 'seeing' the spirit communicator, clairaudience as 'hearing' the spirit communicator and clairsentience as 'sensing' the spirit communicator.)

PRECOGNITION

Precognition refers to the acquisition of information about an event before it takes place. We can anticipate the future and get it right. The weather forecast says it's going to rain and it does – but nobody would say you were psychic just because you knew this. But sometimes it is possible to glimpse the future spontaneously. Most anecdotal reports of seeing the future come from waking visions or dreams that come true, but parapsychologists need something measurable. Using cards as an example again, precognition would be demonstrated by the ability to predict the order in which cards were dealt from a pack, with shuffling carried out only after the prediction had been made.

PSYCHOKINESIS

When Uri Geller amazed TV viewers by bending spoons or D. D. Home levitated himself in front of the Victorian public, they were demonstrating psychokinesis. *This is defined as the power of the mind to manipulate matter without any known physical means.* In a laboratory this can be tested by willing the fall of dice from a mechanical shaker or influencing the numbers randomly generated by a computer.

So there you have it – everything nicely packaged in a scientific way. But, as so often with paranormal phenomena, these definitions can easily get muddied. For example, sometimes when I'm demonstrating my psychic gifts to an audience I will endeavour to give the recipient the six numbers that they wrote on their lottery ticket last week. The odds of getting this right are nearly 14 million to one so it stands as a good proof of the powers of the mind. If they look at or remember their numbers then my prediction could be thanks to *telepathy*. If they have a ticket with them and don't know the numbers on it then it could be *clairvoyance*.

However, I believe that this particular demonstration has nothing to do with either telepathy or clairvoyance, for I am mediumistically in contact with a spirit person who simply tells me the numbers through *clairaudience*. My attempts at *precognition* of next week's

numbers are dismal, however, as I've never won a cent. And as for influencing the balls coming out of the machine with *psychokinesis* – well I'll keep trying!

There are some things that perhaps we're not supposed to know as they may interfere in the laws of cause and effect (karma).

how the brain's psychic powers work

Since the birth of philosophy people have debated whether mankind is primarily a spiritual or a material being. Scientists generally prefer to believe that our consciousness and sense of self are a product of the incredible chemistry of the brain: we are mortal beings. Religionists and philosophers like Descartes and Swedenborg take the opposite viewpoint: we are spiritual beings who have descended to matter and will continue beyond death. The two beliefs are diametrically opposed, and it is difficult to bridge the gap between them.

Moreover, the human brain is designed with a similar paradox. We don't have one brain – we have two. And they think in entirely different ways.

Even with the twentieth century's amazing advances in science the human brain is still an incredible mystery. It requires a fifth of our blood at a rate of 1½ pints a minute to fuel it, uses 20 per cent of the body's total oxygen requirement, and has an estimated 100 billion nerve cells, with every one linked to ten thousand others. Even the brain of a fly is more powerful than today's largest computers when it comes to seeing, moving and reacting to stimuli. Without doubt the human brain is the world's most complex living structure and we are only now taking the first hesitant steps on the very long road to understanding how it works.

Is there amongst this incredible living structure some evidence to suggest where psychic awareness comes from? There is no definitive answer but the brain's structure and activity may reveal a few clues.

Our brains have three main components: the brain stem, at the base, that controls the main life-processes such as digestion, sleep, breathing and heart activity; the cerebellum, at the back of the head that is responsible for maintaining posture and fine muscular co-ordination; and the cerebrum, the biggest and most sophisticated part, that controls the higher thought processes. The cerebrum's crinkly surface is covered by the cortex, a grey rind only a few millimetres thick that neuroscientists believe generates consciousness.

The cerebrum has two lobes connected by a network of half a million nerve axons called the *corpus callosum*. Surgeons discovered that if this neurological bridge is cut it can cure severe epilepsy. Psychological studies of these patients has revealed some peculiar facts about the nature of awareness. The left eye connects to the right brain lobe and the right eye connects to the left brain lobe. If one of these patients was shown an apple with left eye and an orange with the right, and asked what he had just seen he would say an orange. However, if asked to write with his left hand what he had seen he would write 'Apple'. The left and right brains were acting independently. This led to the discovery that the two sides of the brain have very different functions: the left cerebral deals with language and reason and the right with insight and recognition. In other words one side is logical, the other intuitive.

Today's world demands that we develop and use the left brain. We are taught to reason, discriminate, dissect, categorise and verbalise our thinking. But many argue that we should learn to use the right cerebral. This intuitive mind may be the source not only of intuition but latent ESP abilities as well.

The Limits of Reason

The benefits of scientific thought are obvious but the cost has been that we have exiled 50 per cent of our potential consciousness. The intuitive mind has become the dark side of ourselves that we ignore, repress and even fear. And we do this at our peril. We can repress this half of ourselves but its powers will continue to manifest and press upon our awareness. Repressed inner forces can turn nasty,

creating neurosis in an individual or fuelling overwhelming instinctive movements in society at large. Nazism, for example, appealed directly to these instinctive and neglected psychological powers. It re-animated the old Teutonic myths and symbolism that had for so long lay repressed in the German unconscious and burst into the world with terrible fury. The Second World War was a reflection of mankind's soul at war with itself.

Primordial man may have thought in a completely different way to us. He would have been more intuitive and relied on his right brain functions. He may have been aware of subtle natural forces around him such as the magnetic pull of the Moon, the smell of water, the earth's power or the energy fields of plants and people. His own logical mind in its infancy would be 'heard' by him as an independent voice from the gods. He may have been more perceptive and psychically aware, but his life was ruled by superstition and myth. He had the insight of the dream but not the clarity of logic.

The quest for wholeness

Neither empirical science nor the intuitive perception of archaic man is the final answer. A fully integrated individual harmonises both the logical and intuitive aspects of himself. A mystic who rejects logic and discrimination becomes a self-deluded fool. A scientist who rejects intuitive insight becomes a sterile materialist. A whole person draws from the best of both worlds, accepting the intuitive voice yet testing it with the sword of reason.

Psychic perception comes when we integrate the lost self of the right brain. It is an insight that comes to us through our intuition. And millions of people from diverse cultures are taking up this quest for expanded awareness and inner wholeness.

The third eye

Psychics, Hindu yogis, and the philosophers Descartes and Herophilus propose that in the centre of the forehead is a psychic

centre – popularly known as the 'third eye' – through which psychic visions are 'seen' and which is the spiritual centre of our soul. Is there a part of the brain that could account for this organ of second sight?

We do have a real third eye called the pineal gland that lies roughly in the centre of the brain and horizontal to the perceived position of 'the third eye'. In the early stages of man's evolution the pineal gland was once an eye but is now buried deep within the brain. In many modern-day birds, reptiles and animals it lies immediately under the scull and like an eye is sensitive to light. The Tuatara lizard of New Zealand still retains this primitive eye at the centre of its scull. The 'eye' positioned in the cleft in the centre of the lizard's scull even has a pigmented retina, a lens and a transparent membrane. As the pineal gland is sensitive to light it is understood that it governs the cycle of sexual reproduction to coincide with the seasons.

The pineal gland manufactures a chemical called melatonin through the action of a hormone upon serotonin – the chemical messenger (neurotransmitter) which helps nerve cells (neurons) communicate across the connection gaps between them (synapses). It is believed that serotonin is an important chemical in the generation of consciousness and there is encouraging evidence to confirm psychics' belief that this pineal third eye is our spiritual centre. It may be proved in the future that psychics have an unusual serotonin level. (It is also interesting to note that psychedelic drugs such as LSD and mescalin are chemically similar to serotonin and may inhibit its production. Serotonin and melatonin may be the reducing valve described by Aldous Huxley which limits the information entering consciousness.)

BRAINWAVES

Using an electroencephalograph (EEG) scientists are able to detect brainwaves through electrodes attached to the scalp. These show the mental activity of the patient. In our normal waking state we generate *beta* waves and these are seen during active thinking, and problem solving. They are increased by anxiety. *Alpha* waves, however, are produced when the patient is relaxed and passive, and considerably

increase during meditation. *Theta* waves are also found during meditation and seen when the patient is on the verge of sleep. *Delta* waves are present during deep sleep.

Many psychics will meditate before attempting ESP and there is some supporting evidence to suggest that the resulting alpha wave state of consciousness fosters psychic powers. You may have found that your own psychic insights take place during moments of calm relaxation. It has also been suggested that psychics use a combination of alpha, beta and theta brain rhythms. They sustain the meditative state beyond the act of meditation and infuse it into waking awareness. An amazing discovery by Maxwell Cade suggests that psychic healers can impose their brainwaves on their patients but further study will need to be carried out before this is accepted into mainstream science.

INTEGRATING THE PSYCHIC SELF

Artists, musicians and writers understand the power of the intuition. Their inspiration sometimes seems to come from 'outside' of themselves. William Blake felt that his poetry was inspired by disincarnate angels, Rachmaninov composed in a trancelike state, Robert Louis Stevenson dreamed the story *Doctor Jeckyll and Mr Hyde* and even the great physicist Albert Einstein acknowledged a higher power influencing his work: 'The most beautiful and most profound emotion one can experience is the sensation of the mystical. It is the source of all true science.' Even Sigmund Freud, the dogmatic father of psychology, noted in 1921: 'If I had my life to live over again, I should devote myself to psychical research rather than to psychoanalysis.'

Most artists, and some scientists experience this transcendent 'other world' feeling that comes with inspiration. When listening to music have you ever become lost in the inspiration, almost taken over by it? A similar inspirational sensation can overtake a psychic, particularly when working with trance or channelling.

It will come as no surprise to learn that it has been found that many acclaimed psychics have an artistic background. The thinking patterns

are similar: artists and psychics harmonise with the intuitive self. Studies have found that psychics tend to be particularly aware of colour, they are often temperamental, extravert and sensitive.

I would anticipate that many of you reading this book have an artistic gift or appreciation. Psychics and artists come from a similar stock but the difference is that the psychic's inspiration is more than creative – it contains clairvoyantly received information that can be checked.

The psychic personality

Psychics come from all walks of life, but research has shown that many psychic people have certain dominant personality traits. Also there are many misconceptions associated with psychic abilities. These are dealt with below.

Gender

I have written many articles for the press about the psychic experiences of ordinary people and in consequence I get a large postbag. Most of the people who write in saying they have had a psychic experience themselves are women. Surveys confirm that women tend to report and to have more ESP experiences than men, and the general assumption is that women are the more psychic of the sexes.

In reality, the data shows only that women are more willing to talk about psychic experiences than men. A wide range of laboratory experiments have shown that men and women have equal psychic ability. The public's misconception probably stems from society's attitude to the sexes. Women are seen as passive 'receivers' and men as dominant 'senders'. During the Victorian era, when it was socially unacceptable for middle-class women to work, setting up as a psychic was a convenient way to earn extra money. Psychics can quite easily earn a part-time income but even today with the

growing interest in all things paranormal it is hard to earn a full wage from psychic consultations. Rightly or wrongly men are still the family's main breadwinners so there are still more women working as psychics than men.

Age

Some experiments, particularly by Dr Ernesto Spinelli of Surrey University, have shown that children appear to have superior ESP abilities to adults. However, the experiments were conducted in the form of a game which itself may be more productive of good results than the clinical laboratory setting that adults have to work in. Children however, are more trusting and don't censor their clairvoyant impressions. They also tend to be more extravert, which as I have said is a quality associated with psychic abilities. Children may show better ESP abilities not because they are necessarily more psychic than adults but because they are spontaneous and receptive.

Clearly an open-minded approach is conducive to good ESP. As far as I know, there has been little research into elderly people's ESP abilities. Certainly many psychics and mediums I know are still working well into their eighties.

Belief

If sceptics are present when I'm giving a psychic or mediumistic demonstration it can sometimes, but not always, cause a block to the flow of the information that I'm relaying. Most psychics agree that it is much harder to work with sceptics.

Disbelief in your own abilities can also block the flow of ESP. In laboratory tests by Dr Gertrude Schmeidler in 1942 it was found that sceptics scored lower than average results in card-guessing experiments. If they had absolutely no ESP ability then you would expect them to make an average score but their scoring consistently below average suggests that somehow they have suppressed their natural ESP powers to support their own intellectual convictions.

Personality

Most authorities now agree that extravert personality types score better in ESP tests. This may have something to do with brain activity. Tests involving amphetamine and barbiturate drugs that speed up and slow brain activity appear to influence ESP ability but the evidence is scanty.

It has been suggested that extraverts get on better with the experimenter than introverts and that this may be a contributing factor. The evidence, however, is inconclusive. On a personal note I have found that, with my own work, the psychic flow is far more accurate if I like the person I'm working with. It has also been shown that highly neurotic personalities score badly in ESP tests (and again I find them harder to work with if giving a sitting) but often perform better when working in groups.

Culture

It is assumed that certain tribal cultures, like the Australian aborigines or the North American Indians, have an innate propensity for psychic ability. It appears that psychic gifts flourish in societies that accept psi abilities as part of everyday experience. Any psychic who has worked in theatres or with groups will agree that an atmosphere of acceptance accelerates the psychic demonstration.

Intelligence

IQ, it has been found, has nothing to do with psychic ability. It is perhaps a little unfortunate that many good psychics and mediums are also uneducated: they provide the sceptical opposition with so much ammunition.

Trauma

Some psychics have claimed that their abilities, and particularly

psychokinetic abilities, have started after a severe emotional shock or physical accident. This is probably the exception rather than the rule but Felicia Parise a Russian PK expert who could move objects claimed that her gift appeared after a bereavement, Uri Geller's spoon-bending powers came after receiving an electric shock, and healer Matthew Manning says that his mother received a severe electric shock when she was carrying him.

Furthermore, many ordinary people who have been resuscitated from the brink of death and seen a glimpse of the afterlife, claim that the experience has triggered ESP ability in them.

What use are psychic powers?

One of the most frequent questions that TV chat-show presenters ask Jane and myself is "So what *use* is this psychic ability that you have?" It's a difficult question to answer in a short sound-bite. "Laboratory ESP experiments are intriguing but what relevance do psychic powers have to everyday life?"

Perhaps the best way to answer these questions is to look at why people seek a consultation with a psychic and to give a few case examples. Sitters come from every walk of life and for a multitude of reasons. They may want to communicate with the dead, know the future, or hope to understand strange experiences that they've been having themselves. Some seek healing and others come for guidance on their spiritual or material pathway. The remainder of this chapter looks at these motives.

Emotional counselling

A psychic's role is often similar to that of a counsellor or psychologist. At times of emotional crisis a psychic may be able to offer the sitter guidance through a period of turmoil. Of course we can't wave a

magic wand and make difficulties disappear but we can help the client see their problems from a new, and perhaps better, perspective. Sitters often want the psychic to tell them what to do, but the more therapeutic route should be to help the person make their own decisions based upon the emotional issues you have explored with them.

A good psychic can usually get to the root of an emotional issue immediately. Without asking leading questions, they can touch upon key problems that may never have been shared with anyone else before. Broken relationships, fear of rejection, worry, child abuse, suicide and depression are the sort of subjects we find ourselves dealing with every day. I believe, and am told, that the work we do helps people. If you want to work as a psychic adviser you must be prepared, and have the empathy, to tackle all sorts harrowing emotional problems.

PREDICTING THE FUTURE

The main reason that most people come to see a psychic is to find out about the future. Many fortune-tellers have no psychic gift at all. Without an oracle, such as the Tarot, to help them they are at a loss to see past, present and future scenarios. Some fish for information, read facial expressions or make general statements that could apply to just about anyone. A psychic, however, uses skills of precognition.

The psychic must first establish a body of proof that relates to situations already known by the sitter. If he's good he may be able to describe your childhood, where you live now, name names and tell you what you've been doing prior to the sitting. Only when psychically perceived proof of the past and present have been established should the psychic endeavour to predict the potential future. If the perception of the past is accurate then the precognition of the future is likely to be as accurate.

I remember telling one woman that the inside of her garage was covered in green paint. She told me that I was completely wrong: the garage was fine. But when she got home and looked inside the

garage she discovered to her horror that while she was away a tin of green paint had fallen from the shelf and covered everything. I had seen the short-term future with accuracy, and my long-term predictions also came to pass.

A psychic helps the sitter read the map of the future. Some things, like the green paint, may be unalterable events but most can be influenced by free will. Again there's the 'wave a magic wand and make everything better for me' mentality. Sitters must be encouraged to take responsibility for their lives. The future holds many pathways from which we must choose. The psychic helps the sitter to plan a route that leads to good fortune.

You may have had a flash of insight yourself or dreamed of a future event that's come true. At first visions may come unexpectedly and sometimes give unwanted, perhaps disturbing glimpses of impending disaster. So remember this important fact: what you are seeing is only a potential future; destiny is not completely predetermined. We have free will and can change the future. We'll go into detail about this in Chapter 3.

Proof of life after death

A psychic who communicates with people from the afterlife is called a medium. Mediums are the most highly skilled of psychic practitioners and mediumship is an ability possessed by very few individuals. It is said amongst psychic circles that one in a hundred people can develop a psychic gift but only one in a million can become mediumistic.

Proof that there is a continuation of life beyond physical death can be a great comfort for the bereaved. The primary objective of mediumship is to prove that the personality survives bodily death. This is achieved by a telepathic blending of thought with the communicator from the spirit side. The medium relays the information that is shown him and builds up a character profile of the communicator. If the medium is clairaudient and can hear the spirit voice then they may be able to give the full name and hard facts about the spirit person's life when on

earth. The love that pours forth over this psychic bridge can change people's lives. It proves that death is not an end but the entry into a new realm of existence. And of course, the philosophical implications and the shift of material priorities this creates for the sitters is of paramount importance.

Your own experiences of the spiritual realms may have come as a sudden and unexpected insight. The 'dead' can communicate to ordinary people through dreams, in meditation or when they are distracted. Some people smell the aftershave or perfume of a loved one (described by mediums as a psychic breeze) or maybe you 'see' or 'hear' the communicator. Although these communications pass between the spirit's mind and yours you may, if your faculty is particularly acute, actually see the communicator, not as a ghostly form, but as if they were a living person.

Spiritual insight

There are many people today who are asking spiritual questions that traditional religion fails to answer. Why are we here? What happens after death? What is reality? Is there a purpose to my life? Also the precarious predicament of a world civilisation living under the threat of thermonuclear war, irreversible pollution, ozone depletion, overpopulation and a science gone mad inventing genetically engineered Frankenstein species of animal, plant and germ has made us reconsider our role as custodians of the planet. We are bombarded with information, great leaps of discovery are happening but we find nothing to satisfy our spiritual yearning.

The information explosion has resulted in us no longer believing blindly in what the priests or scientists tell us. We want to find out the answers for ourselves and, as sages have always urged, the best place to look is within ourselves. The Buddha said 'seek out your own Salvation' and that is what many people are doing today through what has been dubbed the New Age Movement.

Astrologers tell us that there is a great shift happening in the heavens as we enter the Age of Aquarius and that there will be a

bright new era ahead after a period of world-wide crisis. A great spiritual awakening is taking place. Millions are turning to meditation, ancient traditions and the mystical systems of old. And mass psychic awareness is growing from these seeds.

You may have already spontaneously become aware of your latent psychic abilities – a faculty that all people can use if they want to. If so, you are part of a great evolutionary leap in consciousness that is happening right now and will continue to unfold as we pass the millennium. In the following chapters we'll look at ESP in detail, its spiritual implications and ways that you can use it to transform yourself and others.

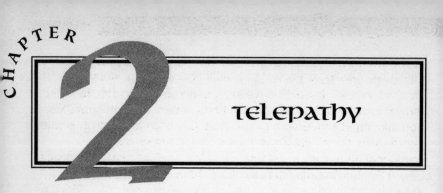

TELEPATHY

Can you read thoughts?

- *Does your pet respond to your mental commands before you voice them or know when you're about to arrive home?*
- *Have you ever tried to phone a friend at exactly the same time they've tried to phone you?*
- *Have you ever sensed that someone you know is in distress even though they are miles away?*
- *Do you know what mood a person is in even before you see their face?*
- *Have you ever taken an instant dislike to someone and found out later that your initial gut feeling was true?*
- *When you fell in love did you and your sweetheart say the same things at the same time or finish each other's sentences?*

If you can answer yes to some or all of the above questions you may have the psychic skill of telepathy. In the previous chapter we defined telepathy as the transmission of information from one mind to another without the use of language, body movements, or any of the known senses. It is a mind-to-mind communication.

how telepathy works

Whether it be your pet, friend or lover if there is a natural empathy between you then this mind-to-mind communication happens more

easily. My own experience suggests that telepathy happens most effectively on a feeling level. This may be a remnant of an old survival instinct. It would have been important to be able to sense danger around an individual or to know if they were on your side. If you take an instant dislike to someone this is an instinctive warning signal. Also, the pineal gland, which I have suggested is the traditional 'third eye', is associated with sexual reproduction cycles. This telepathic bonding may therefore have a survival function associated with falling in love and choosing the right mate. Once a strong telepathic bonding has been established the information communicated between the individuals increases beyond the feeling level to include shared imagery and thoughts.

Telepathy has other useful survival functions. Ancient man believed in the interconnectedness of all life. His tribal society was regulated by the clairvoyant insights seen in the shaman's dreams, animals' spirits were ceremonially coaxed to help with the hunt, and plants would 'tell' the medicine men what healing properties they had. And there are also many civilised people who believe that telepathic communication can take place between humans and plants. One of the most famous was American horticulturist Luther Burbank, who stated that he could make a plant conform to a pattern by the use of loving will-power. Reverend Franklin Loehr believed that his prayers would make his plants grow, and scientist Cleve Backster wired plants to a lie detector and found with his experiments that they responded to mental threats that he projected to them by telepathy. And the tabloid press had a field day when Prince Charles confessed that he talks to his plants.

In the days before language mankind may have had a rapport with nature that we can barely begin to imagine. A telepathic link between tribal members would certainly have improved upon communication by grunts, gestures and facial expressions. Renowned anthropologist Margaret Mead believed this and said that in some primitive cultures she had seen evidence of 'special supernatural powers'. Furthermore it has been suggested by the psychiatrist Jan Ehrenwald that telepathy is a pre-language survival aptitude and occurs between mother and infant during the dependent period before the child acquires language. Once verbal

communication is mastered, telepathic communication is no longer fundamental to survival, and the ability is either suppressed or lost. In short, telepathy is an ancient skill that functions at a subconscious, non-verbal level of consciousness. It is an intuitive way of thinking, originating perhaps from the right brain lobe, and similar in content to dreams.

A TV EXPERIMENT

I was asked by Anglia Television in Norwich to conduct an experiment in telepathy for one of their light entertainment shows. It was decided that we would divide the audience into two sections. One group would send a target image drawn on a large board by Anglia's graphic department; the other group would receive the image.

My first step towards a successful experiment was to talk the audience through a simple technique to open the 'third eye', unconsciously activating the pineal gland deep in the brain. Once the audience were in the right frame of mind I then asked the 'senders' to imagine that they were transmitting a stream of light toward the other group, who envisaged themselves receiving this flow of energy through the centre of their forehead. The 'receivers' were blindfolded so that they could not see the other side's facial reactions, and the picture was then held up in front of the 'senders'.

When the presenter questioned the receiving group we first asked how they *felt* about the image: what was their emotional reaction? The overwhelming response was that it was a sad image although some said that it was sad but had a humourous element. Some said that there was a person or child involved and many identified that the colour white was important. And one embarrassed audience member described the target drawing exactly – a crying child urinating into a white lavatory!

Now I would be the first to admit that this type of experiment lacks the discipline of a controlled laboratory experiment, even though the programme-makers were careful to ensure that no cheating went on. (I even saw the presenter cross the words 'Well that didn't work did it?' off her script.) However, it does illustrate what I was trying to demonstrate about how telepathic impressions are transmitted: most of the audience was correct with their *emotional* response to the target picture, some perceived the important colour accurately but only one got a direct hit by describing the picture's content. Telepathy works best as an emotional response and in a cheerful atmosphere.

Think about your own telepathic experiences: You probably didn't hear words but would have sensed a communication between yourself and another. You may have just 'known' that someone was in trouble, for example, or acted upon an impulse, such as phoning a friend at a critical time, without knowing why you had to do so.

Scientific experiments with telepathy

The Apollo missions to the Moon were, in the now clichéd words of Neil Armstrong, 'one small step for man but a giant leap for mankind'. And less well known was that another giant leap was secretly being attempted during the Apollo 14 journey: to prove that thoughts could be transmitted and received from the Moon. A former US Navy pilot, Edgar D. Mitchell was the sixth man to walk on the Moon. He said of his experience: 'It was an explosion of awareness, an "Aha!" a "Wow". Instead of an intellectual search there was suddenly a very deep gut feeling that something was different.' On his return he announced, to the dismay of NASA, that he had conducted secret experiments in telepathy.

The 1971 experiments in ESP left Mitchell with a lifelong interest in the subject. He resigned as an astronaut only two years after his Apollo mission to found the Institute of Noetic Sciences to study ESP and human consciousness. 'There seems to be more to the universe than random, chaotic, purposeless movement of a collection of molecular particles,' said Mitchell. 'On the return trip, gazing through 240,000 miles of space towards the planet from which I had come, I suddenly experienced the universe as intelligent, loving, harmonious.'

Since making his first telepathy experiment in 1971, Mitchell has, over the years, tried out many New Age ideas: yoga, gestalt therapy, transactional analysis, rolfing, rebirthing, psychodynamics, acupressure and acupuncture, shaitsu, meditation and 'a lot of breathing techniques'.

In fact nearly all the squeaky-clean astronauts who returned from the Moon had a hard time adjusting to Earth life. Buzz Aldrin, the second man to set foot, achieved press notoriety because of his womanising, Colonel James B. Irwing, the eighth, formed a fundamentalist Baptist Church and spent a great deal of his time searching for biblical artefacts, and in particular Noah's Ark, and Charles Duke, who landed the Apollo 16 lunar module Orion near the Descartes crater on 20 April 1972 became an evangelical Christian minister. But for Edgar D. Mitchell the Moon experience was a prelude to a lifelong interest in telepathic experimentation.

The experiments that Mitchell tried involved a traditional guessing system using Zener cards. These were invented by J. B. Rhine and Karl Zener from Duke University and consisted of a set of 25 cards, each printed with one of five simple geometrical symbols – a star, a circle, a square, a cross, and wavy parallel lines. The purpose of the experiment was for four 'receivers' on Earth to guess the sequences of the cards telepathically 'sent' by Mitchell during his scheduled rest periods.

Unfortunately Apollo 14's lift-off was delayed by 40 minutes, which altered the timing of the rest periods, and only four of the planned six experiments were undertaken. They proved inconclusive.

Mitchell's experiments with telepathy were the sequel to a massive body of work undertaken by J. B. Rhine started in the 1920s at Duke University. Rhine was inspired by previous attempts by such people as Charles Richet, John Coover, George Estabrooks and William McDougall to prove or disprove psi abilities statistically, and as a young man he had been particularly impressed by a lecture on Spiritualism given by Sir Arthur Conan Doyle, author of the Sherlock Holmes stories.

For his ESP experiments Rhine recruited subjects from the university campus. They were mainly selected at random and included people who made no claims to psi abilities. Repeated tests were carried out using the Zener cards, with the deck being shuffled each time, to reduce the possibility of a chance good result. Often the 'sender' and 'receiver' (also called the 'percipient') would be located in separate buildings. Over and over again the Zener card experiments were successful, with correct guesses well above the level of chance.

According to the theory of probability, chance would have indicated that the receiver was likely to score five hits in a single run of 25 Zener cards. Nine out of 25 correct guesses was considered 'statistically significant', giving an approximately 20 to 1 variation from chance. Experiments with eight psychically gifted subjects pushed these results well above chance. In a total of 85,724 trials they achieved 24,364 hits, which is 7,219 more hits than would be expected to occur by chance alone. Experiments with the psychic divinity student Hubert Pearce, undertaken at the faculty by J. Gaither Pratt between 1933 and 1934, saw the odds rise to 10,000 billion billion to 1 against chance.

The results that I've quoted are just a small part of the huge number of experiments that Rhine conducted during his lifetime. They caused unprecedented antagonism in the scientific community – and still do. But Rhine's meticulous work was just the start of a massive investigation into ESP throughout the world. Many have verified Rhine's results and introduced new systems to eliminate any methodological weaknesses, and new techniques have been tried using random number generators and moving video images. An open-minded person closely studying the results of this multitude of experiments cannot fail to accept that telepathy has been proved to exist. J. B. Rhine died in 1980 at the age of 84. Many consider him the father of the science of parapsychology. His integrity, zeal and scientific method encouraged others to develop his work, yet the scientific establishment still refuses to accept his findings and only a handful of universities are prepared to fund parapsychological research.

How to amplify your telepathic perception

Activating the aura

Surrounding our physical body and extending for about 12 feet in all directions is a field of life-force energy known as the aura. Many people naturally sense this energy, which has sometimes been referred to as the human atmosphere or morphic field. For example, you may know that a person is in a bad mood by the vibration that they are projecting through the influence their aura has on you. With training this sensing can be developed into an ability to see the aura, which appears at first like a gentle heat haze of light. Bright colours, rays and fibrous filaments of light can also be perceived by the adept. When people are talking to each other the aura is seen as flowing from one person to another. If two people are arguing then it is possible to see how the auric lights conflict with one aura dominating the other. We live in an ocean of interacting life-energy. Some people may deplete your auric field, others may recharge you – there is a vast flow of cosmic energy continually ebbing between us all through which telepathy can take place.

This is not a new idea. The ancient Egyptians, Greeks and Romans drew haloes around the heads of their gods or priests, as did the painters of Christian saints. Hindu yogis have for centuries described the aura in their holy texts. In the late 1930s the Russian scientist Professor Semyon Kirlian developed a photographic technique to capture this 'bioplasmic energy' on a photographic plate. Kirlian photography was refined further to produce colour images, and a friend of mine, Guy Mason, has developed a startling new technique that shows moving images of the aura on video film. It is particularly intriguing when the aura of a healer's hands are photographed. When they are asked to extend their healing powers, bright blue and orange lights are seen radiating from their fingertips.

Within the aura are seven concentrations of energy that psychics believe are the source of ESP. Eastern yogis have known about these for centuries and call them the *chakras* – which translates from the Sanskrit as 'wheels'. They are spinning vortices of life-force that link the physical body with the auric body.

The chakras have their counterparts on the physical body centred near the endocrine glands with a corresponding position horizontal to them along the spinal column. In the Western system each chakra has a coloured light associated with it, moving from red at the lowest centre through the colours of the rainbow to violet at the highest. At the base of the spine is the first chakra; its colour is red and it functions as the powerhouse driving the other psychic centres. In yoga this base chakra is recognised as the seat of the kundalini energy that, if released by special techniques, travels like an uncoiling snake up the spine and to the crown of the head. It is the key to many of the yogis' superhuman powers and fuels their spiritual journey towards enlightenment.

The second chakra, the sacral centre, is located just below the navel. Its colour is orange and it binds the auric body to the physical. Next comes the solar chakra that lies just below the rib-cage. This yellow centre is the storehouse of our psychic energy that can be tapped when needed. In the centre of the chest lies the green heart centre, which is the seat of the emotions. Through this centre the psychic perceives the emotional state of his sitter.

The three higher centres that follow interact together to result in ESP abilities. At the top of the throat is a chakra with a bright blue light. It is believed that this centre is responsible for clairaudience or hearing spirit voices. In Victorian seances participants would see a substance called ectoplasm build a voice box over the throat centre and a communication could be made directly with spirit entities that could be heard by everyone in the darkened room. On a psychic level it is the link to the inner voice of your higher self. When this centre is activated the psychic experiences a slight constraint in the throat area.

In the centre of the forehead lies the 'third eye' centre which we mentioned in Chapter 1. The colour associated with it is indigo but

when the centre is opened it appears to the inner eye to be composed of many flowing colours and hues. Also when this centre is activated there is a feeling of three 'psychic bands' stretched around the head. Celestial visions of a clairvoyant nature can be seen through this chakra. Some may be fantasy but others reveal verifiable information that can be perceived only through clairvoyance. Some yogis claim that the third eye is also the centre of our will.

Lastly, at the top of the head lies the crown centre. This is our opening to the cosmic power. It spreads outward like a thousand-petalled flower of ethereal light spreading its petals into the infinite. Meditating on this centre brings an awareness of our highest spiritual nature. If this is united with the energy flowing from the base centre, it brings cosmic consciousness. It is through the crown centre that the spirit leaves the physical body at death.

The inner Alchemy

The spiritual energies of the soul are focused upon the seven chakras. An earthy person will have the focus of their energies on the base, sacral and solar chakras, whereas a person capable of great feeling and expression may have the heart chakra as their main energy focus. Intellectual, creative and spiritually orientated individuals will draw their energy to the throat, forehead and crown chakras.

Psychic development depends on the activating of the three higher centres and circulating the cosmic energy between them. It is possible to bring about an inner transformation in which the gross energies of the base centre are gradually transmuted into the subtle energies of the throat, forehead and crown. An inner alchemy takes place in which the gross sluggish lead of the lower energies is transformed into the radiant gold of the highest.

Assuming that the scientific premiss of reality is correct, it is impossible to change one element into another by chemical means. However, the alchemists may have understood their secret experiments to be symbolic of powerful spiritual transformations to the soul. The Swiss psychologist Carl Jung identified in the alchemists' texts many archetypal symbols representing psychological change. The Russian spiritual teacher Georgei Ivanovitch Gurdjieff saw the human body as the 'vessel' that changes lower into higher energies. And Taoists describe, in books such as *The Secret of the Golden Flower*, how the alchemical goal is achieved by the circulation of the auric light during meditation.

Moving the cosmic energy

The transformation of the auric energy necessary for psychic development is activated by the power of the mind. Thought, like a philosopher's stone, can move the currents of the aura. Healers do this when they project a love-saturated mental picture of good health to their 'patient'. With it flows the auric current channelled from the inexhaustible cosmic source. Most healers focus this energy through the hands but it will flow just as easily by the power of the mind. Where thought goes, life energy follows.

PRACTICE

We can heal our own auric body in this way and use the same auric powers to fuel psychic perceptions. To do this we must first activate the aura. To increase your psychic attunement imagine that your aura is expanding. One by one the chakras open like flowers of light, from the base centre through to the crown. In particular, visualise a brilliant light opening in the centre of the forehead. Now imagine that you are flooded with golden light from above and your whole auric body is shining with incandescent light. Feel the aura expand outward. (A full explanation of this technique is described in my *Psychic Workbook*.)

By activating the aura in this way your latent psychic abilities will be activated. When you have finished experimenting, imagine that the lights in the chakras from the third eye to the base centre gradually fade as the flower petals close. With the crown centre still open imagine a golden light washing through you from the top of

the head and out of your fingertips and toes clearing away any unwanted impressions. Finally close the crown chakra and pull the aura in. Visualise yourself wrapping up in an imaginary black velvet, hooded cloak to shut the centres down. It is important to close down in this way after psychic work or others may unconsciously drain your life energies.

A TELEPATHIC EXPERIMENT

Open the aura in the way I have just described and try to communicate a picture between yourself and a friend who has also opened their aura. Ask your friend to think of a scene or event. If the subject matter is emotionally charged the image will be easier to communicate. The person communicating the target image should visualise that the image is flooding their aura and that their auric light is expanding and influencing the aura of the receiver. Imagine your two auras expanding and merging.

You, as the receiver of the communication, should imagine that your aura is absorbing the impressions being sent. Next, try to 'see' the scene in the third eye at the centre of the forehead. Describe all of your impressions and particularly the feelings that you are experiencing. With practice you should be able to perceive both the emotional and visual content of your friend's signals.

When you have finished and compared the results, reverse roles and try again. This intriguing experiment can quickly yield results that may surprise you. When the experiment is over, it is important to close your chakras down in the way I described earlier.

Psychometry

We are continually projecting telepathic thought into the world around us. Although telepathy can travel through walls and over

any distance some of these thought vibrations are absorbed into our environment. Just as water 'remembers' the vibration of a toxic chemical in homoeopathic medicine, so matter 'remembers' the thought vibrations that have been impressed on it. The life-energy visible in the aura can be transferred to inanimate objects.

Visit a church and you will sense the atmosphere of peace; go to a slaughterhouse and you will feel the horror in the air. When you buy or rent a property are you not aware of its atmosphere? Have you not made a decision about where to live because a place *feels* right? You were using your psychic powers to 'pick up' the thoughts that had become telepathically embedded in the fabric of the building and you inwardly replayed these messages from the past.

If this ability is developed it is possible to read the thought vibrations left on any object held. The psychometrist can describe the characteristics, thoughts and feelings, and life history of the owner/owners of the object. This ability is called psychometry, which literally means 'soul measurement'. (Strictly speaking, psychometry is a clairvoyant faculty as the information is being perceived from an object and not directly from the mind of another person. However, these impressions have been initially implanted by the projection of thoughts outside of the body so I include it in our study of telepathy.)

Some of the earliest investigations into this phenomenon were made in the mid nineteenth century by Dr Joseph Rodes Buchanan of Covington Medical Institute. His experiments proved that some of his students could distinguish different chemicals when they were wrapped in thick brown paper. Also he found that many were able to relate an accurate history of the object and describe its previous owners.

Psychometrists have often been employed by the police. Dutch psychic Peter Hurkos used psychometry to help with the Sharon Tate murder investigations in 1969; psychometrist and housewife Dorothy Allison from New Jersey helped the police trace more than 26 missing people; Gerard Croiset held a hammer used in a murder and correctly identified the culprit; and today Nella Jones combines psychometry with mediumship to help the British police with their investigations.

During a consultation I often use psychometry to 'link' with the sitters' vibration. By holding an object it is quite easy to describe the person's character from the feelings I sense from the object and I can describe events from the person's life by interpreting the images I see in my 'third eye'. Psychometry is most accurate if I don't know who the owner is so that I'm not distracted by the facial expressions and reactions of the sitter. A profile is built up by first describing the owner's character, then events from childhood, followed by the history of their life to the present day.

Psychometry is a useful psychic stepping-stone. Once the psychometric link is established I can move on to extend it to the sensations I feel emanating from the sitter's aura, and then expand this further to link with their spirit friends or to look into their future. Psychometry is a cornerstone in psychic development. It is comparatively simple to teach and can be mastered by most open-minded people.

PRACTICE

Try psychometry yourself. Ask a friend to hand you a watch or item of jewellery that has been the exclusive property of someone they know well. Simply hold the object, close your eyes and talk about the owner. Describe the feelings you get about the personality of the owner. Then describe any pictures that just pop into your head. Don't censor your thoughts or try to make sense of them. No matter how silly you feel, say whatever comes into your head. Try also to describe the childhood and life history of the object's owner. Say anything that comes into your mind. When you analyse the session afterwards you will find that a large percentage of what you say is relevant to the object's owner. With practice your accuracy will continue to increase.

Another interesting experiment to try, which I've also demonstrated on live television, is to project a specific picture onto a quartz crystal. Quartz crystals amplify psychic signals. Ask your friend to think of a scene and holding the crystal to their third eye, project the image into it. You now hold the crystal to your own forehead and

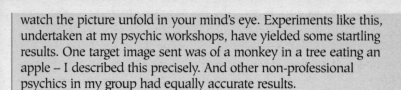

watch the picture unfold in your mind's eye. Experiments like this, undertaken at my psychic workshops, have yielded some startling results. One target image sent was of a monkey in a tree eating an apple – I described this precisely. And other non-professional psychics in my group had equally accurate results.

Telepathy and dreams

The greatest obstacle to psychic perception is the logical mind. You will note that I've advised you, when trying ESP experiments, to accept everything that comes into your mind without censorship. When we are asleep our waking mind cannot filter out disconnected and extraneous impressions and feelings. And it is during sleep that many people have telepathic experiences.

Some of the best-known dream telepathy experiments were started by New York psychiatrist Montague Ullman in the 1950s and further developed from 1965 at his dream laboratory within the Department of Psychiatry at Maimonides Medical Centre in Brooklyn. Ullman would note when a sleeping volunteer subject was dreaming (which can be detected by rapid eye movements beneath the sleeper's eyelids), and then by telephone instruct a 'sender' located several miles away to open an envelope and begin concentrating on a target picture. These target pictures were selected for their emotional intensity, vividness, colour and simplicity and the 10 volunteers were recruited with a positive attitude towards ESP. The subject's dreams were then compared to the target picture being sent by telepathy. There were many misses but amongst the material were some inexplicable hits where the sleeping subject described dreams with startling resemblances to the target pictures.

During sleep we have unrestricted access to the powers of the right-hand brain – the source of many ESP experiences. This is a time when telepathic communications can take place without interference from the restrictive logical mind. For example, a large-scale telepathy

experiment was set up in 1971 by the Maimonides dream laboratory with the audience watching a pop concert by the Grateful Dead. Malcolm Bessent, an English psychic, slept at the lab while the audience were shown a projected image of a picture chosen at random. They were than asked to mentally transmit this picture to the sleeping Bessent 80 km away. One picture shown was an illustration of the chakras with a yogi levitating, which Bessent correctly described, referring to 'nature's energies', levitation, sunlight and the spinal column.

PRACTICE

You could set up smaller-scale fun experiments with your friends. If for example there is a group of six, five at a time could be 'senders' while one takes a turn as the 'receiver'. The five senders can each be given an identical coloured picture (colour photocopies are not expensive nowadays) which they pin on their bedroom walls and attempt to transmit over a week during sleep. Select a picture that contains vivid, colourful and emotional imagery. The receiver, who is not shown the target picture, writes down his dreams every morning and brings his notes when the group next meet. Some receivers from my own weekly psychic development group have often scored a hit for the emotional content and colours of the target and their dreams have occasionally featured the target picture precisely.

An alternative is for one person to be the sender and the other five to be the receivers!

In the next chapter we will look at how ESP abilities can be used to look into the future.

clairvoyance and precognition

Can you see distant events and the future?

- *Do you ever know what somebody is going to wear before you meet them?*
- *Have you ever 'seen' a distant event taking place as it happens?*
- *Have you ever told someone where to find a lost item even though you had no clues as to its whereabouts?*
- *Have you ever dreamed of an event that's come true or experienced déjà vu?*
- *Are you lucky at gambling or able to anticipate the numbers in roulette or the fall of dice?*
- *Have you ever cancelled a journey because of a gut feeling that something bad was going to happen?*

If you can answer yes to some of the above questions you may have the psychic skills of either clairvoyance or precognition.

Telepathy, as we have already explained, is the acquisition of information by one mind from another. Clairvoyance, however, is the acquisition of information about an object or event, and precognition is the acquisition of information about events that lie in the future.

Clairvoyance

Clairvoyance would be present if the psychic was able to read the pages of a closed book, give the sequence of a shuffled but undealt pack of cards, or see events taking place at a distance. The target information to be 'seen' by clairvoyance should not be known by anyone else or it could be claimed to be received by telepathy.

The average person sees the world around them only with their physical eyes but clairvoyance is a way of perceiving things beyond the scope of the eyesight. For example, the clairvoyant inner vision may see through walls or witness events taking place at some distant location. Some psychics believe that clairvoyance happens to people who are able to get out of the physical body and 'see' by means of the astral body. They shift their centre of consciousness outside of themselves.

I have explained how everybody has an aura that can blend with the aura of another. You may have already proved this to yourself by practising the telepathic auric blending technique I showed you in the last chapter. I believe that everything has an auric field and that all life blends into a great sea of life vibration. Life is interconnected by a mycelium of living energy and wherever we are, we are connected to every part of the universe. In other words every part contains the whole, and we can all connect to this spiritual Internet and through this super-conscious state realise that we are omnipresent beings.

Remote viewing

One form of clairvoyance that I find particularly intriguing is to describe a distant location without ever having seen if before. Parapsychologists have called this ability 'remote viewing'. I have tried a number of experiments of this nature at my psychic groups with a startling success rate.

For our experiments I would ask a member of the group to give a house name and I would proceed to describe it. I would 'see' the location in my mind's eye. At first from above, as if I were floating over the location, and then at close quarters going through the front door and describing the rooms and people who live or work there. Sometimes only a map reference was given. In most of our experiments I was able to describe the target site accurately. We also found that many other group members were soon able to get good results with a little training.

To test that I wasn't reading the mind of the person who had selected the target location we randomly selected map references and then checked out the location afterwards. We continued to get accurate results. Of course we weren't 100 per cent accurate but sometimes the little details described proved beyond doubt that what we were saying was more than lucky guesswork or vague descriptions that could be applied to anywhere.

You could try this for yourself. Ask a friend to hide an object somewhere and you can describe the object itself and the environment where it's located. Again it's best to get the feelings right first: 'I feel it's fluffy, soft, loved and tattered. It's near somewhere wet, dark, muddy, cold, green, prickly.' In this case the target object is a child's teddy bear hidden in a holly bush by a river. For successful remote viewing it's important to describe the sensations you feel before progressing to the scenes observed or names of streets heard. Sensing is the foundation of good clairvoyance upon which we can build our visual and auditory psychic perceptions.

In order to rule out telepathy, parapsychologists invented a number of machines to test clairvoyant abilities. These included Random Event Generators (REGs) which would choose numbers or objects in a truly random way or switch on coloured lights as the radioactive strontium 90 in the machine's heart decayed. The problem with guessing fixed targets like cards, numbers or random pictures is that the subject matter is dull and a bored clairvoyant soon loses interest.

The accuracy of their response declines. 'Free response targets', in which the clairvoyant is asked to describe video footage or to sketch what he senses about a randomly selected location, yields far better results.

One of the masters of remote viewing was American psychic and artist Ingo Swann, whose remarkable talents were tested by the American Society for Psychical Research in 1972. He drew substantially accurate pictures of objects that were placed on a suspended platform above where he was seated. When the CIA discovered that the Russians were experimenting with similar remote viewing techniques and to direct their clairvoyants to look inside top secret US installations, they employed Swann to head a team of clairvoyants to psychically spy on Soviet defence projects. Given only the latitude and longitude Swann and his team gave such accurate intelligence information about target sites that his team enjoyed substantial government funding for many years. Swann says that his viewers would 'see' nuclear material with 'a greenish glow something like the Cryptonite from Superman stories'.

On a more spiritual level, absent healing can be sent through a similar 'remote' technique. I received hundreds of letters from people asking if they could be included in my psychic group's absent healing list when I briefly mentioned the subject in an article I wrote. (The core group has included a GP, a plastic surgeon and nurses.) Everyone who wrote was sent a letter and asked to attune themselves to us at the time designated to channel healing energy. In some cases all we had to work with was their name and a brief note about the illness they had.

It was a strange sensation when the appointed time came. The thoughts of hundreds of people seemed to fill the room. Using a special visualisation technique and calling upon the powers of the radiant spirit beings, we asked that God's power be put behind our efforts when the absent healing rays were sent. Letters soon started coming in from people saying that their health was improving. And happily my father's X-rays revealed that his bone cancer had considerably improved. Where thought goes, healing energy follows.

PRACTICE

Try absent healing yourself. Sit in meditation and picture the person who you want absent healing to be sent to. Imagine them healthy and well. Never dwell upon the negative aspects of their condition. Think only positive healthy thoughts. Next picture them in a beautiful setting such as a celestial garden or in a forest filled with flowers. Picture the colours around you and send these colours as a bright ray of light. Ask in your heart that the angelic beings add their healing energy to your winged thoughts. Pour your loving thoughts out to the distant subjects and know that the invincible power of God will guide the healing rays.

PRECOGNITION

When you develop your psychic abilities you may find that your life starts to change. Unusual coincidences may confront you and guide you to people of like mind. You may feel an inward prompting to change your lifestyle and destiny may throw challenges and opportunities for change into your path. A psychic person taps into another level of reality where time and space take on a different meaning and the resulting transformation of the self influences the events attracted into their destiny.

LOOKING TO THE FUTURE

We assume that time travels in a straight line like an arrow pushing ever onward. But what is time? Does it have a beginning and an end? Can it go backwards? We are aware of the present and remember the past, but can human consciousness also extend into the future?

Great thinkers such as Saint Augustine, Galileo, Sir Isaac Newton, Albert Einstein and Stephen Hawking have wrestled with the peculiar

enigma of time. It appears so simple but when we analyse it time is almost impossible to explain. Modern physicists theorise, using Einstein's equations, that if a spaceship could travel between two black holes in space then it would move through time. They talk about hyperspace and cosmic wormholes that tunnel through space-time leading from one region to another. And nuclear physics has now discovered strange subatomic particles that appear to travel backwards in time or be in two places at once. The arrow of time is flying in disarray.

Experiments with precognition

When my wife Jane and I appeared every Friday with Paula Yates on TV's *The Big Breakfast* as the resident psychics, our task was to predict the coming week's newspaper headlines. Not vague, woolly forecasts but specific events – Paula Yates was a tough customer to work with. Yet our accuracy, as reported by startled newsmen, was over 85 per cent. We even surprised ourselves sometimes. Among our correct predictions were various transport accidents, including the El Al air tragedy in Holland.

Of course Jane and I are not the only people with this precognitive ability. Many ordinary people have this gift as well. And sometimes it has saved their lives.

The strange case all at sea

One of the problems with proving that an event has been 'seen' through precognition is to decide whether it was perceived by a genuine psychic sense or whether the correspondence between a premonition and actual event was the result of an extraordinary coincidence.

For example my grandfather's second cousin, 17-year-old cabin boy Richard Parker, was shipwrecked on a boat called *Mignonette* in 1884. With him were Captain Dudley, Edwin Stephens as mate and Edmund Brooks as hand. The four castaways were stranded for 16

days in the South Atlantic 1,600 miles from land. On 25 July 1884 the crew drew lots to decide who would be sacrificed for the sake of the others. Richard Parker, who was delirious from drinking sea water and knew nothing about what was going on, was killed by his starving shipmates and eaten.

Forty-seven years before this event shocked the Victorian public, writer Edgar Allen Poe published in 1837 a fantasy called *The Narrative of Arthur Gordon Pym of Nantucket*. The short story tells of four men who were shipwrecked and after many days privation drew lots to decide who should be killed and eaten. The cabin boy drew the short straw – and his name was Richard Parker!

Even today this story seems to attract weird coincidences. I could list dozens but the strangest happened to my father Don Parker. Three Spanish language students were staying with my parents. Over supper, as is the family custom, he told them the grisly tale. The television was on in the same room and to the surprise of everyone it showed a regional short-story programme about the cannibalism that took place on the *Mignonette*. My father explained how the story seems to attract weird coincidences and about how Edgar Allen Poe's story had predicted Richard's demise.

All three girls went white. 'Look what I bought today,' said one. She reached into her shopping bag and pulled out the complete works of Edgar Allen Poe. 'So have I,' said the other two girls in unison. Independently that same day they had each bought the same book containing the Richard Parker story!

Had Edgar Allen Poe seen the future when he wrote his gory story or was it just another extraordinary coincidence similar to the many that so many people report happening when this strange tale is told? The story is such a coincidence that some authorities, including Arthur Koestler, think that it may signify some psychic phenomenon and not be a coincidence at all.

Another disaster at sea that attracted strange coincidences and seemingly genuine precognition was the tragic sinking of the *Titanic* on her inaugural voyage from my home town of Southampton to New York at 23.40 hours on the night of 14 April 1912. This terrible disaster, that happened 700 kilometres off Newfoundland, was a

tragedy foretold. In 1898 author Morgan Robertson published a novel telling the story of the demise of a supposedly unsinkable ocean liner named *SS Titan*. Incredibly, apart from the coincidence of name, Robertson's story featured a long list of similarities with the real events that coincided with the *Titanic*'s sinking.

He described the sailing of a gigantic steamship from Southampton on its inaugural voyage that hit an iceberg and sank. The *SS Titan* was almost a clone of the White Star Line's *Titanic*. Robertson's *Titan* was 70,000 tons (the *Titanic* displaced 66,000 tons) measured 800 feet (the *Titanic* was 882.5 feet) transported 3,000 passengers (the *Titanic* carried 2,207) and like the *Titanic* was driven by three propellers.

Morgan Robertson was writing at a time when the technology to build such a ship did not exist. His story was pure speculation. One of its main themes was that the arrogant owners of the *Titan* were so convinced of its unsinkability that they provided only 24 lifeboats for the 2,500 passengers. The *Titanic* sank with a loss of 2,224 passengers and crew. There were only 20 lifeboats – half the number required.

An intriguing study of precognition associated with the *Titanic* disaster was conducted by Ian Stevenson, a psychiatrist at the University of Virginia. He found 19 instances of apparent ESP associated with the tragedy. The psychic experiences were reported from people who had loved ones aboard the ship and others with no apparent connection. Many people postponed their trip for no obvious reason but J. Connon Middleton, a London businessman, reports that he cancelled his trip because he dreamed for two nights in a row that the ship was sinking while people struggled around it. A female stewardess who escaped onto an overloaded lifeboat recalled concentrating on her 11-year-old daughter during the ordeal. At the same time, the daughter – in New York – was overcome with a 'strange sense of doom' about her mother and dreamed that her mother was in a lifeboat that was in danger of capsizing.

Perhaps the most famous person to report a precognition of the event was novelist Graham Greene. 'One the April night of the *Titanic* disaster, when I was five,' he wrote in his autobiography, *Sort of Life*, 'I dreamt of a shipwreck. One image of the dream has

remained with me for more than sixty years: a man in oilskins bent double beside a companion-way under the blow of a great wave.'

From the examples we have looked at it appears that Edgar Allen Poe, Morgan Robertson, Graham Green and the passengers of the *Titanic* all experienced precognition. Before we examine how this faculty can be used by fortune-tellers we will first consider some of the theories associated with it, and in particular how dreams can sometimes reveal future events.

SERIALISM

J.W. Dunne was a distinguished man of science and professor of mathematics. To his dismay he found himself repeatedly dreaming of events before they happened. Many were of trivial things such as being chased by a horse but others concerned events of world-wide importance, one being the eruption of Mount Pelee in May 1902, which destroyed St Pierre, the main trading centre of the island of Martinique, and killed 40,000 people. But soon Dunne was to meet other people whose dreams contained foreknowledge and his initial scepticism began to fade. He began to suspect that people in general may have dreams of future events. Applying the methodology he had learnt from mathematics, he embarked upon a lifetime study of precognition. In 1927 he published his basic conclusions in his bestselling book *An Experiment with Time*.

Keeping detailed dream records and comparing dreams with friends, Dunne proved to himself that in sleep, and sometimes in day-dreams, the mind can roam beyond the bounds of space and time. He found also that prophetic thoughts can be engendered in the waking mind if it is kept in a state of receptivity. Upon his experimental work Dunne evolved his theory of temporal serialism. He argued that if time was a fourth dimension then the passage of time must itself take time. If therefore time takes time there must be a time outside of time. He called this 'time 2'. 'Time', he said, 'is not a straight line, like a stretched cord; it is more like a tangled skein of wool.'

Most of our life we live in 'time 1', which is synonymous with the passing ordinary moments of everyday life. But during sleep a part

of our personality (observer 2) can slip into this other dimension of time and experience events in the future which are communicated to our ordinary self (observer 1). Investigations led Dunne to conclude that under certain circumstances past, present and future events were accessible to consciousness and that during dreams we can enter this fourth dimension of space-time.

The belief that during dream/sleep we are no longer captive to the present is not a new idea. Tales of prophetic dreams can be found in ancient Egyptian papyri, the Old Testament and religion and folklore throughout the world. Perhaps Dunne's greatest achievement was not his somewhat grandiose theory of serialism, but his bringing to the public's attention that everyone is capable of precognitive dreaming. A simple yet effective method to test this possibility – and you should do this yourself – is to keep a dream diary by your bedside and record dreams immediately on waking.

I have recorded my own dreams over many years and note that there are many instances where they have revealed future scenarios. As with all psychic perception, the feelings are the foundations upon which visual and auditory information is built. Sometimes, like an infuriatingly incomplete jigsaw puzzle, the dream contains one part of a prophetic insight. My conclusion is that only the *potential* for the future can be seen. The future can be changed. The psychic reads the map, but free will decides the path we take.

Divination and prediction

Attempts to predict the future date from earliest times and are common to all cultures. The first astrologers came from ancient Babylon, Sumaria and Egypt, the alphabet of the ancient Greeks is the foundation of numerology, the rune oracle originates from the Vikings, a version of the I Ching was first used 5,000 years ago in early China, and the symbolism contained in oracles such as the Tarot embraces Christian, pagan and oriental religious references. The future has a distant past.

Many influential people have consulted fortune-tellers. The Oracle at the temple of Delphi pronounced that the philosopher Socrates was the wisest man alive and was perhaps responsible for the jealousies that forced his suicide. Croesus, King of Lydia, asked an oracle whether he should invade Persia and was told that a great nation would be destroyed. They were right, but unfortunately for him it was his own empire that fell. Michel de Notre, better known as Nostradamus, was consulted by the royal families of the medieval world. American author Mark Twain was in 1895 facing bankruptcy, with debts of over $90,000. When told by the famous palmist Cheiro that he would receive a great sum of money when he reached the age of 68, he was sceptical. But in November 1903, at the age of 68, he was unexpectedly offered a contract with Harper, the publisher, which cleared his debts and gave him an income of $100,000 per year. To the joy of the tabloid press the famous to this day continue to consult psychics for advice.

CONSULTING THE ORACLE

Methods of divining the future can be broadly broken into two approaches: mechanical interpretation according to a system; and the use of a system as a vehicle for ESP. They are dealt with below.

The acclaimed Swiss psychoanalyst Carl Jung proposed that everything in the universe is connected, hence the way in which the Tarot cards fall or the position of the planets in our horoscope has a bearing upon that particular moment in time and can be interpreted as an oracle for potential coming events. His theory of synchronicity was based upon the old alchemical precept, 'as above, so below'; every part is considered not in isolation but in relation to the whole. He asserted that everything that takes place at a particular moment of time has the qualities of that moment, and that all events taking place at the same time are connected. Everything in the universe is linked, including, in the case of the Tarot divination system, the client's question and the random selection of cards.

Jung used the word 'synchronicity' to indicate what he termed 'the equal significance of parallel events'. In particular he applied his ideas to the ancient Chinese oracle of the I Ching or Book of Changes, first translated into English in 1882. The simplest method of consulting the I Ching is to throw three coins six times to form one of 64 hexagrams. These are different combinations of six broken and unbroken lines that symbolise the interaction of female (yin) and male (yang) cosmic forces. When the hexagram is known, the querent is directed to a particular passage of Chinese philosophy and wisdom that is relevant to the circumstances that they are experiencing.

By throwing the coins the querent connects himself to the great network of relationships between people, things and events. Carl Jung called this 'an acausal connecting principle', which, in very simple terms, means that some events happen without one causing the other; they just happen to happen at the same time. The fall of the I Ching's coins, the Tarot card spread or the fall of the runes are 'meaningful coincidences' that reflect present and future events.

To use any of the systems mentioned above requires no psychic skills. The professional consultant knows the tools and rules of their trade inside out and their interpretation is a combination of knowledge of symbolism and intuitive assessment. An oracle read at face value can give interesting information but cannot compare to the psychic use of precognition.

Count Louis Hamon, better known by his pseudonym Cheiro, became during the 1890s the world's most famous palmist, and his bestselling books are still popular today. He was the darling of Victorian society, sought out by the rich and famous. He accurately predicted to King Edward VII that he would die in his 69th year. He foresaw the impending difficulties that led to Oscar Wilde's ruin. When he visited Russia in 1904 he told the Czar that he would be deposed after a calamitous war between 1914 and 1917. And for Lord Kitchener he predicted, over twenty years in advance, that he would die by drowning in 1916 unless he avoided all forms of sea travel. Kitchener went down on the *Hampshire* in 1916. With predictions like this it is surprising that Cheiro was so popular.

The accuracy of Cheiro's predictions extends far beyond the information marked out in the lines and mounts of the hands. From the examples above and from the thousands of others that have been documented it is clear that he was using ESP faculties.

An oracle such as the palms can either be read at face value according to tradition, or in conjunction with precognition. Cheiro used the latter method, as do all psychics worth their salt.

For oracular purposes the hand is interpreted by examining its shape, the length and shape of the fingers, the fleshy mounts beneath the fingers, thumb and wrist, and the major and minor lines crossing the palm. Together these provide information about the character, talents, and past and future life of the sitter. But the psychic palmist will see more than the lines and mounts could ever tell him.

Have you ever shaken someone's hand and felt that something about them was not quite right? You may have been doing a business deal and felt as soon as your hands touched that this person could not be trusted. When a palmist touches his sitter's hand the vibration of the person influences their intuition. You will remember how we did the same thing with an inanimate object in the psychometry experiment earlier. Also the auric powers combine and additional information flows telepathically into the psychic's consciousness. In addition the precognitive faculties of the psychic senses the past and future conditions of the sitter as their intuitive awareness links into the fourth dimension of time-space that Dunne described in his theory of serialism.

For example the palmist looks at the heart line that crosses the palm horizontally from below the little finger. He notes that it has many islands and breaks, indicating that the person will have many problems in their emotional life. He notes also a number of fine lines crossing the life line, that runs from above the thumb to the wrist, to suggest the timing of these events. He also sees that the person has an overdeveloped mount of Venus, by the thumb, indicating that they are of an over-passionate nature and that this could be the cause of some of their problems. From this, and of course from the many other markings, the palmist can give a

comparatively detailed account of the sitter's emotional life. However, when a psychic's intuition builds on this structure more information is revealed. They may be able to describe in detail the people who've influenced the sitter's emotions, give the exact dates when relationships started and finished and see potential opportunities for the future. They can look into the sitter's inner hopes and fears and see the strengths and flaws of the personality that should be strengthened or controlled. A good psychic can touch the very foundations of the sitter's traits that instigate a life of good or bad fortune. The palm gives clues but ESP does the rest.

I am personally a little suspicious of palmistry as I believe that everyone can influence their destiny for the better. If I read a client's hand I prefer to stress that the palm reveals only the potential challenges and opportunities. The future is not absolute. Whether the palm holds bad omens or your stars bode ill, in the final analysis the future's what you make it.

If ESP is applied to the Tarot, a reading can leap from the superficial to the specific. When cards are shuffled and a spread laid out the random cards fall according to the laws of synchronicity. They reflect, as Carl Jung asserted, the qualities of that moment in time and have a bearing on the future. So, for example, you note that the card of the Devil lands in the position in the spread relating to the querent's environment. Traditionally the Devil indicates the baser instincts of lust, anger, deceit and jealousy. The interpreter of the cards will understand this to mean that these negative forces are challenging the querent from his environment. Adjacent cards will reveal additional information about the problem, the people involved and potential ways of addressing the situation.

But interpretation of the cards is only a part of the process of reading a Tarot spread. As with palmistry, the psychic Tarot reader becomes attuned to his sitter and receives information through the aura. Telepathic insights reveal the emotional causes of trouble and the reader may be able to describe the characteristics of the people causing it. Events and scenarios may unfold within the psychic's third eye centre and provide information that could never be gleaned from the cards alone. When an accurate description of the

current conditions is given, the psychic can progress to look into future events using his precognition. Once the vibration link is firmly established between himself and the sitter his intuitive insight will link to future conditions. If he describes the past and present correctly the odds are that his predictions of the future will be correct as well. The cards, palms, runes, etc., are only part of the oracle. They are catalysts that trigger precognition.

Some advice

My training in ESP has come from a mediumistic background. A fundamental belief that nearly all mediums hold is that a person should take personal responsibility for their life. This includes the fact that we have free will. However, many people who visit psychics want to be reassured about the future and often expect them to somehow make all their problems disappear. They want to delegate their responsibility to use their own free will. Someone else, they hope, will make the decision for them. This is clearly psychologically unhealthy.

Fortune-telling and precognition should always be seen as *advice*. In my opinion there is no predestination, only potentials that can be glimpsed by ESP. Without free will we are no better than machines. The psychic should encourage, inspire and advise clients to take the helm of the ship of destiny. If you are hoping to use your own psychic skills, be aware that you have a tremendous influence on people's lives. Use your ESP gifts with love. Guide people, help them, teach them to face the challenges of life, and stimulate them to enter the future with courage and hope.

4

PSYCHOKINESIS (PK)

Can your mind control matter?

- *Have you ever influenced the fall of dice when playing board games?*
- *Does machinery go wrong when you're angry or upset?*
- *Can you influence the shapes of clouds when you gaze at them?*
- *Do pictures fall off the wall, computers malfunction or your watch keep stopping for no apparent reason?*
- *Do some people feel an electric shock when you shake their hand?*
- *Have you ever moved an object just by the power of your will?*

If you can answer with a yes to some of the above questions you may have psychokinetic abilities.

Psychokinesis (PK), as explained in Chapter 1, is the power of the mind to manipulate matter without any known physical means. It is a hybrid word derived from the Greek for 'mind' and 'motion'. One day there may be a simple explanation of this paranormal ability to bend spoons, levitate objects or influence computers by mental powers. It may be that some people have an unusual quirk to the electrical or magnetic fields generated by their bodies, or science may yet discover entirely new forms of energy.

Consider, for example, the case of 14-year-old Angelique Cottin of La Perriere, France, who in 1846 generated what appeared to be an uncontrolled electrical charge. For 10 weeks her touch sent heavy furniture flying across the room, compasses danced wildly in her

presence and those around her could not touch any object she had held. This 'high voltage syndrome' may also explain cases of spontaneous human combustion where a person bursts into flames for no apparent reason. Some authorities believe that the body's unusual electrical effects account for PK phenomena.

Many parapsychologists offer other explanations and suggest that it is possible for the human brain to interact directly with the environment. They have observed an increase in the brain's alpha wave activity during experiments with subjects who exhibit PK. Also, theta waves are present during trance, and delta waves could be projected as part of the defence mechanism. However, as basic physics tells us, to exert a force on an object some form of energy has to be used. PK theorists have speculated that heat or sound may supply the necessary energy and that the power is drawn from the environment or even the sitters themselves. Early levitation experiments indicated that everyone present had lost a few ounces in weight. Wherever this energy comes from, it is clear that the mind somehow focuses energy like a laser beam that concentrates benign light energy into a powerful force. Once concentrated the PK energy is directed at an object to make it move, bend or levitate.

Parallels in PK phenomena are also drawn with the strange behaviour of subatomic particles. Events in this microworld are often unpredictable. German-born physicist Helmut Schmidt claims that certain psychically gifted observers can affect events at the quantum level. If matter can be manipulated by mind in the microworld, argue parapsychologists, perhaps the same can happen in our macroworld. A basic law of physics is that no object can be moved without expenditure of energy. PK may draw its energy from the quantum world.

Alternatively there may be a non-material component to the universe, and man is in part a non-physical being, and capable of exercising far greater control over his environment than is assumed by science. More and more people have discovered these new powers that seem to defy the laws of nature and few scientists dare face up to the implications and problems that psychokinesis poses. PK, if proven beyond question, would turn current scientific thinking

on its head. In its simplest form psychokinetic powers can move objects or bend spoons. Its most advanced manifestation produces phenomena that challenge our fundamental understanding of reality.

Miracle-makers

Psychokinesis is a cornerstone of religion. We read in the world's holy books stories of people who had a miraculous control over the material world and could transcend the laws of nature. Early civilisations, without the scientific means to test or investigate these miraculous powers, worshipped these supermen as gods. (St Joseph of Copertino, for example, floated into the air whenever he experienced religious rapture. These flights of ecstasy would happen almost daily in front of many witnesses including the philosopher Leibniz.) The Industrial Revolution heralded the advent of an unprecedentedly materialistic era, yet at the same time strange things started to happen in the seance room. Even today we still hear of people who display incredible powers over matter as miraculous as those described in the Bible, Koran or Bhagavad Gita.

Daniel Dunglas Home (pronounced Hume) was born in Scotland in 1833, and during his lifetime he became the world's most acclaimed medium. As well as being able to communicate with the dead he could perform astonishing feats. Tables and heavy items of furniture, such as a grand piano, would float to the ceiling or across the room when he was present. He could levitate himself, and in broad daylight and in front of a team of sceptics including notable names such as Lord Adare, the Lord of Lindsay and Captain Wynne, he was seen to float across the room, out of one upstairs window and back in through another. Many scientists also saw Home's feats and signed depositions bearing testament to what they had witnessed.

Home's abilities astonished onlookers: he could wash his face in red-hot blazing coals, make himself inches taller or shorter, communicate with the afterlife mentally or with raps and in trance he would speak languages that were unknown to him. Poltergeist activity was ever present around him as was controversy. Many, like

Sir William Crooks, the famous Victorian physicist, and the socialist theorist Robert Owen believed that Home's powers were remarkable and true, whereas author Charles Dickens and the poet Robert Browning considered him a fake. Yet D.D. Home was never proved to have been fraudulent and, although he mixed in society's highest circles, he refused to accept money for his incredible demonstrations. He lived and died in near poverty.

Home claimed that his powers came not from himself but from the spirits of the dead and the Victorian world saw the advent of hundreds of Spiritualist mediums with pronounced psychokinetic powers. Some were frauds of course but many like Home were hard to discredit. Italian medium Eusapia Palladino, who was born in 1854 and orphaned at the age of 12, displayed psychokinetic effects from an early age. Unfortunately she would sometimes take short-cuts and on a number of occasions was caught cheating. Despite this fact many researchers believe that this character flaw cannot account for the many genuine displays of PK she demonstrated. These included the ability to levitate heavy furniture and materialise spirit forms. Her powers were tested by many sceptical researchers, including the famous Charles Richet, who attested to the reality of her remarkable abilities.

Austrian mediums Rudi and Willi Schneider were tested by the arch-sceptic Harry Price in a controlled environment and under strict supervision. The two brothers could make objects move, produce ectoplasmic masses, rapping and table tilting.

Many 'physical mediums' such as Helen Duncan and Mrs Guppy could materialise apports and produce from their bodies a white substance called ectoplasm. This would transform into the face or bodily form of a recognisable deceased person. Ectoplasm is a white, luminous, misty substance that is generated by the spirit world from the physical body of the medium. It usually pours from the medium's mouth and builds from the floor upwards into the form of the deceased communicator. Sometimes only a face, hands or voice box will materialise but if the power in the seance is high, the whole spirit body will materialise. Powerful mediumship produced forms that were as solid as you or I. Sitters in these darkened circles could talk with and even touch their dead loved ones!

In society at large science was banishing religion and mysticism to history, but in the secret back rooms of Spiritualist circles a strange new model of reality was unfolding.

Table-tilting

Edith Piaf, the famous Parisian street-singer made no secret of her interest in Spiritualism and often took part in the popular parlour game of table-tilting. It tapped out a cryptic message: 'March 22, aeroplane falls, everyone dead.'

Edith Piaf realised that she was booked on this very flight and ordered that none of her company should travel. The aeroplane crashed into the sea killing all 67 passengers on board.

Table-tilting was practised extensively by the early Spiritualists and results can be obtained quickly. A small table is placed in the centre of a circle of seated people and everyone places their hands lightly on its top. The group leader, usually a medium, asks if there is a spirit who wants to communicate. The table will move or a rap will be heard.

The table usually rocks from side to side and messages can be tapped out when the legs hit the floor or from the raps emitting from it. One knock for yes and two for no. Detailed messages can be obtained by designating a number for each letter of the alphabet: A=1, B=2, C=3, etc. In this way messages can be communicated directly from the dead using the collective psychokinetic powers of the people present.

I've experimented in this way with one of my own psychic groups. Sometimes nothing but gobbledygook was spelt out but on some occasions the 'spirit communicator' spelt out their name and address before death. On one occasion it tapped out 'Robin will live at Walnut Cottage.' Robin, one of the circle members, now lives at Walnut Cottage.

But there can be problems. I've spoken to skilled mediums who have had bad experiences with this technique. Some messages can be embarrassing, frightening or deeply disturbing. One group I know

saw their heavy table split in two. Similar difficulties can be associated with ouija boards and planchettes. I know someone who had used the ouija board and it told them that all five people present would die soon. A week later one was involved in a fight and died of head injuries. Another died a few months later from pneumonia, and a third took his own life. The two survivors still live in fear.

Fortune-telling that employs psychokinesis is very unreliable. The movements of the table or the apparent accuracy of the messages spelt out on the ouija board can be very convincing. Spiritual forces can work through these techniques, and there are many examples within the Spiritualist and SPR's records to suggest this. But the sitter's inner fears and hopes can influence the 'communication'. Collective telepathy manifesting through psychokinetic phenomena can be a wild, uncontrolled power.

A fascinating example of how thoughts can influence the psychokinetic powers witnessed in table-tilting was demonstrated by the Toronto Society for Psychical Research under the leadership of Iris Owen. In 1972 the group decided to manufacture a fictional seventeenth-century ghost whom they gave the name Philip. They gave him a colourful history. He was an English aristocrat whose beautiful wife Dorothea was frigid. Secretly Philip took a gypsy mistress, Margo, whom he hid in the gatehouse of his home at Diddington Manor in Warwickshire.

But Dorothea found out about the clandestine affair and had Margo burnt at the stake. In despair at losing his only true love the fictitious Philip threw himself from his castle's battlements leaving his wandering ghost to seek his beloved Margo through the seance rooms.

The Toronto group met weekly to discuss Philip in the hope of conjuring up his ghost. They adopted the relaxed, cheerful atmosphere that British researcher Kenneth J. Batcheldor had proposed encouraged PK phenomena. If the conscious mind is lightly engaged, he argued, then it freed the unconscious to combine with the mental energies of others to produce PK. Tibetan Buddhism recognises a similar technique. A prolonged visualisation of a person

or a god can become an entity in its own right. Although originally created only by thought it will take on a life of its own and do the bidding of its creator. Tibetans call these 'beings' *tulpas*, and lamas and magicians warn that a tulpa can get out of its maker's control and become mischievous or even dangerous. Similar stories can also be found in the archives of magic and in Arabian stories about genies.

After a year of patient sitting and meditation the Toronto group started getting results. They experienced table levitation and other PK effects. The imaginary Philip started to communicate. He began to rap loud messages about his fictitious, colourful life through the table-tilting circles. The table could dance up a flight of steps by itself and Philip even performed and answered questions on a Canadian TV show.

The evidence would suggest that Philip was a deliberate group hallucination that somehow took on a life of its own and could display PK. An alternative suggestion put to me by a number of Spiritualists, is that a real, mischievous spirit was obliging the researchers by imitating their manufactured spirit. We can never know the answer for certain.

Scientific studies of psychokinesis

The first systematic experimental approach to psychokinetic phenomena was conducted at Duke University by Joseph Banks Rhine, whose experiments with telepathy, clairvoyance and precognition we considered in earlier chapters. As with his other studies, Rhine chose his subjects from among university students who professed no paranormal abilities.

His experiments with ESP had indicated that in some cases the mind could bypass the senses and know information about the world by some unknown mode of perception. Was it not conceivable that the mind could also bypass the body and interact with the material world? He was inspired by a casual meeting with a gambler at his offices in 1934. The man demonstrated that he could

influence the fall of dice in his favour, particularly when he was excited, confident or anxious to win. Rhine began his own PK experiments with his student subjects.

Using two dice Rhine asked his subjects to throw eight or more. The results proved statistically significant, yielding scores in the first run of 562 tests of odds against chance of 1 in a billion – well above the mean chance expectation (MCE). To eliminate any affect of throwing techniques Rhine tightened his procedures by using both painted and embossed dice, and he designed various mechanical devices to throw them.

PRACTICE

You can try a simple fun PK experiment yourself. First decide on a target number between one and six. Rhine found that higher numbers were easier to obtain than lower ones because of psychological success associations so perhaps you should choose six as your target number. Shake a dice in a cup and concentrate on getting that number. Just as you did with the telepathy experiments imagine that there is a blending between you and the dice. Create a mental rapport. Speak to the dice, either in your mind or out loud. Believe in yourself. Know that you can do it. The right frame of mind and an enthusiasm for the experiment are an important factor in successful PK tests.

Now as you concentrate throw the dice 60 times and note your score. Less than 15 correct and you are not showing PK abilities. Between 15 and 35 is well above average, and over 35 means that you have a mind-boggling influence on the dice.

You may find that your success rate deteriorates if you undertake prolonged experimentation. As with telepathy, clairvoyance and precognition experiments, J.B. Rhine observed that this decline effect reflected the subject's loss of interest which suggests in reverse fashion that something is in operation early in your experiments but missing later. In Rhine's PK tests the drop-off was calculated as occurring at odds against chance of 100 million to 1. And, as with other ESP

experiments, the degree of belief in your powers can prove significant. Rhine found that sceptics again scored below what you would expect from chance alone and may have been exhibiting reverse PK.

Since Rhine's pioneering work thousands of PK experiments have been undertaken in laboratories throughout the world. In Russia during the 1960s the Soviet psychic Nina Kulagina was shown to move objects inside glass jars or boxes. She was also able to create burn-like marks on a British researcher's arm. Ted Serios from Chicago was seen to project images onto photographic film, as did Masuaki Kiyota in Japan. American psychic Ingo Swann used psyckokinetic energy to raise and lower the heat on specially insulated, super-sensitive temperature detectors. Professor Gertrude Schmeidler reported that Swann, was able, from over twenty feet away, to effect slight temperature changes of up to 1 degree. Rolf Alexander of Canada astonished researchers and journalists by demonstrating that he could influence the shapes of cumulus clouds. In England Nigel Richmond claimed that he was able to influence the movement of paramecia, tiny single-celled organisms that inhabit pond water. And of course Israeli-born Uri Geller has bent spoons by paranormal means in research labs throughout the world and in front of millions of TV viewers.

Psychokinesis is coming of age. But the most remarkable PK reports are not coming from the world's labs or as seen on TV shows. PK powers demonstrated by people like Uri Geller intrigue, entertain and challenge scientific preconceptions, but his demonstrations are unlikely to make you reassess your life. PK in the hands of a holy man can bring about a spiritual transformation. I believe in free will and am not a follower of gurus, but in India at this moment a phenomenon is happening that, if genuine, may overturn our concept of the mind's relationship with matter for good.

Miracles still happen

On his deathbed Pope John XXIII is said to have had a vision of a man who would usher in a new Golden Age such as mankind had

never known. He described him as a small, barefooted man with brown skin who would wear a distinctive red robe. Similarly, the great sixteenth-century seer Nostradamus and American prophet Edgar Cayce predicted that a holy man from the east would challenge the major religions of the world as a prelude to a New Age.

Ten years ago few people would have heard of the remote village of Puttaparthi in India's southern state of Andhra Pradesh. Now the attention of millions is focused on this stone and thatched village because of one man: Sri Sathya Sai Baba.

Born on 23 November 1926, Sri Sathya Sai Baba demonstrated remarkable materialisation phenomena from an early age. At the age of 13, after a two-month period of illness and unconsciousness, he announced to the startled villagers that he was an avatar – a teacher sent directly from God. This, he said, was his second incarnation, the previous being as Sai Baba of Shirdi a Muslim fakir who had died in 1918. There would be a third to come, as Prema Baba. Over these three lives he intends to bring the religions of the world together as one brotherhood with universal love as their foundation stone. His philosophy is simple: 'Love all, serve all.'

Most people actively engaged in psychic work or study have heard of Sai Baba. He's not what you'd expect a great man to look like. He is a small, baby-faced man with a distinctive mop of black fuzzy hair similar to the style popularised by guitarist Jimmi Hendrix. And just like the deaihbed vision of Pope John XXIII he is barefooted and wears an orange/red robe. Yet his followers include world leaders such as the former president and prime minister of India, S.D. Sharma and P.V. Narasimha Rao, as well as the ex-president of Italy and the prime minister of Norway. Prince Charles is said to have requested an interview but to have been refused. Isaac Tiger, who donated the proceeds of the sale of the multi-million Hard Rock Cafe businesses to Sai Baba's cause, says of him, 'He is not what he appears to be at all. He is much more dynamic than a little man with furry hair running round building universities and hospitals.' (Sai Baba has established free hospitals and schools throughout India, and the government has accepted his system as a model for a welfare state.) In India he is headline news and his influence is rapidly spreading to the West.

Never before has anyone displayed such remarkable PK powers. The reports coming out of India are mind-boggling. Sai Baba has raised the dead, multiplied food as Christ did at the Last Supper, materialised jewellery out of the air and turned water into petrol when his car ran out of fuel. There are tales of him materialising sweets directly into people's mouths, appearing in two places at once and making a photograph of the face of Christ appear on film. Most of his manifestations have been demonstrated in front of highly respected professional people and are particularly well documented by Dr John Hislop and Howard Murphet.

There are of course sceptics who argue that Sai Baba's miracles are nothing but clever conjuring tricks. The fact that he has levitated in front of hundreds of people or can materialise jewellery from thin air can be explained by single trickery and sleight of hand. But when you read the thousands of testimonials or meet intelligent people whose lives have been completely transformed after an encounter with Sai Baba you soon realise that to trick people on this scale would be impossible. For example Sai Baba will often ask people, 'What do you want?' and many people will ask him to materialise very obscure things: fruits out of season, a perpetual motion watch, a map of the future world, some wood from the original cross, and specific medicines. To keep all this up his short-sleeved robe would be an impossibility.

Knowing that every Rolex watch has its exclusive serial number, an Australian visitor asked the swami to materialise one for him. Sai Baba obliged with a wave of his hand. On his return the serial number enabled the Australian to identify where the watch had been purchased. He asked the proprietor if he remembered who bought it. The owner remembered the occasion well. He could hardly forget the unusual orange-clad Indian gentleman with strange fuzzy hair.

The shop owner was a meticulous man who kept accurate sales records that gave not only the day of purchase but the time as well. Together they checked the records. It corresponded exactly with the time and day that Sai Baba had materialised the Rolex. Sai Baba had been in two places at the same time!

Another intriguing story, and there are thousands, concerns an Australian who visited Sai Baba in the hope that he could cure his wife of terminal cancer. Sai Baba spoke to him saying, 'You shouldn't be here. Your wife needs you. She will be well.' He then tapped the Australian three times on the forehead. The man vanished in front of a crowd of people and reappeared beside his wife's hospital bed in Australia. Baffled by what happened he checked his passport. It was stamped correctly with that day's date yet only moments ago he was in India. His wife recovered.

You don't have to travel to Puttaparthi to experience Sai Baba's miracles. By asking him in your mind Sai Baba will answer your spiritual questions and in some cases perform remote PK miracles. My wife Jane and I read the stories, had lucid dreams about him and listened to many people who testify to the reality of his miracles, so I decided to set him a test to convince me once and for all. I thought of something as obscure as possible and wrote my request down. 'If you're true, show me a green monkey.' Soon after I had an important meeting that worried me greatly. In front of the building was an advertising hoarding showing a soft drink being drunk by a green monkey. I never saw the same poster again.

All over the world there are people who have had similar simple but profound experiences of this nature. Sai Baba's most frequent materialisation is of a healing ash called *vibhuti*. Hindus consider this to be very holy and on a par with the holy sacrament of Christianity. In the *Daily Telegraph* of 6 March 1992 a reporter witnessed vibhuti ash forming on photos of Sai Baba and objects in the room at the home of Mr G. Patel in Wealdstone, Harrow, London. In honour of Sai Baba's 70th Birthday, Mr Patel carved a life-size wooden statue of his guru. As soon as the task was complete, vibhuti ash began to form on the statue's hands, gown and feet. Mr Patel took a photograph of this but when the film was developed it was not the statue in the picture but a photograph of the real Sri Sathya Sai Baba!

Remarkable as these stories about Sai Baba are, they are unlikely to convince traditional scientists until he is tested by researchers under laboratory conditions. Sai Baba considers that this is unnecessary.

'Miracles are my visiting cards,' says Sai Baba, and on another occasion, 'My greatest miracle is Love.' His spiritual teaching and the character transformation it triggers are far more important than the tantalising PK phenomena he displays:

> *For what purpose were you born? Man has been sent into the world to realise the truth that he is not man, but God. The wave dances with the wind, basks in the sun, frisks in the rain, imagining it is playing on the breast of the sea; it does not know that it is the sea itself. Until it realises the truth, it will be tossed up and down; when it knows it, it can lie calm and collected, at peace with itself.*

If we embrace the spiritual principle of unconditional love, says Sai Baba, we too will become godlike and manifest the same incredible PK phenomena. This, he suggests, is the next evolutionary step of mankind.

In the next chapter we will consider some of the spiritual implications of ESP perception.

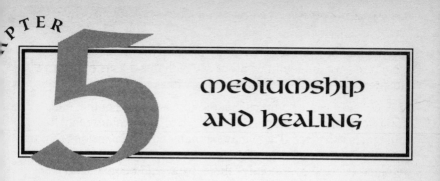

mediumship and healing

Do you use your sixth sense?

- *Do you pay attention to your intuitive thoughts and feelings?*
- *Do you act upon your hunches?*
- *Do you sense a guardian spirit or angel influencing the course of your life?*
- *Do unexpected events or coincidences draw you to people of a similar spiritual persuasion?*
- *Have you ever thought that the material world we see is just a shadow of a far greater reality?*
- *Are you seeking a spiritual perspective to life?*

If you answer yes to some of the above questions then you perceive the world and view reality in ways that are very different from the average person. Most people focus their energy and thoughts on the mundane and material but a person who is searching spiritually realises that there are other planes of existence that we can communicate with from within ourselves. The sixth sense links us with these other worlds.

The ESP faculties we have considered demonstrate that thought is not confined to within the brain. We can communicate telepathically with each other; we can shift our perceptions and see, by means of clairvoyance, environments that are out of the reach of the traditional five senses; we can look into the past and future and the power of our thoughts can even influence the physical world by

psychokinesis. The subjective and objective worlds are not as separate as we think and what we see with our eyes is only part of a much greater reality. There are worlds within worlds.

Science has given us a much greater understanding of the material world yet it has only mapped the fringes of the greater reality that constitutes existence. There may be many other dimensions that we are not aware of and they may be so incomprehensible that, even if we could become conscious of them, we would be unable to understand our experience. If ESP can see beyond the five senses then could it not also 'see' into the heart of the atom, 'observe' the cellular life within our bodies, 'view' other planets, 'communicate' with dolphins, 'receive' messages from distant galaxies or 'talk' with the angels? Some claim to do these things. And many people listen to every crazy fantasy that any over-imaginative 'psychic' or 'channeller' can envisage. Mankind may stand at the threshold of a new spiritual understanding but we must still retain our discernment or we may fall into a metaphysical quagmire.

Now call me old-fashioned, but I need a little proof before I believe every notion I'm told. I am reminded of an incident at a psychic fair when my friend decided to pay to have a reading with a woman who claimed to be able to sketch her sitters as they were in a past life. It sounded very exciting. The childish drawing she produced for my friend showed him as a gardener in Atlantis. 'Well I can't deny it,' observed my friend, 'How can I prove otherwise?' Of course without proof or evidence anybody can claim to be a psychic.

Mediumship

A good psychic gives facts that can be verified. This is particularly important when making a communication with the spirit world. The medium's function is primarily to give evidence to prove that the human personality survives death. Of all the psychic abilities mediumship is the most difficult to cultivate yet the most profound in its spiritual implications.

My wife Jane and I believe that mediumship represents the pinnacle of psychic development. Together, we have demonstrated telepathy, clairvoyance and precognition on TV, radio and in the newspapers but the most important aspect of our work is to demonstrate that it is possible to communicate with another world that is as real as the one we live in now.

To illustrate my point about the importance of giving verifiable facts I now include a testimonial from a person who watched me give a public demonstration of mediumistic communication – Linda Perrin (44), from Poole in Dorset. I could have chosen from many endorsements (and Jane has many too) but this spirit message is easy to verify, as an independent person took notes, and the demonstration took place in front of an audience. Needless to say, I had never met the people receiving the information prior to the meeting that took place at Jubilee Hall, New Milton, Hampshire. Her testimonial is as follows:

> *Craig started his clairvoyant demonstration by saying that an impatient, quick-tempered man was communicating with him and was giving the name Martin Cooper. I put my hand up. Nobody else could place the name and it appeared to be for me.*

> *Craig continued by saying that Martin had thrown all his money away before he died and that he was joking that he didn't believe in an afterlife. And still doesn't now! (Martin had always said that Spiritualism and the like were a load of rubbish.) His death, said Craig, had happened in a shop doorway. It had been sudden and he'd fallen to the floor and banged his head as he did so. (Martin Cooper, a dear friend, had died of a drug overdose. His body was found in a shop doorway and his head was badly bruised.)*

> *Craig went on to correctly describe Martin's other physical ailments, such as the arthritis in his right hand, his stomach condition and that he had a fear of cancer of the stomach. He mentioned that his friend Melanie had his watch that was broken. I checked on this later and it proved to be correct. The watch had broken down a couple of days before.*

Craig said that Martin wanted me to tell his mother that he was alright now and said that there was a lady in Lancashire who still hadn't heard the bad news yet. (A close friend of his lived in Oldham, Lancashire but hadn't returned from her holidays yet.) 'Also,' continued Craig, 'he's telling me to make sure that his scrappy dog is looked after.' Martin and his girlfriend had a poodle dog whose coat had become very untidy. It had recently been given away to friends.

We all really sat up as Craig concluded his communication with Martin. 'They're shaving me,' Craig said. 'Just a minute, Martin says that they're shaving him as we speak. He's not been buried yet! His body's still in the morgue!'

There was absolutely no way that anybody could have known this. Martin had only died the day before and they were preparing his body as Craig spoke.

This example illustrates many of the ESP faculties that are activated when a medium communicates with the afterlife. It could be argued that I had telepathically read Linda Perrin's mind. But how did I know that her friend Melanie had the watch and that it was broken? Linda Perrin had to check this as she had no knowledge of a watch or the fact that it was broken.

The telepathy that takes place occurs not with the person sat in the audience but with the person communicating from the after life. This mental communication between the worlds is impressed upon the medium in three ways: clairsentience, clairvoyance and clairaudience.

CLAIRSENTIENCE

This is the easiest form of mediumship. The medium will sense the character traits of the communicator, know if they are a family member, be able to give their gender and feel what part of the body was responsible for death. It is surprising how much accurate information can be communicated by the spirit person through clairsentience. An accurate character profile can sometimes say far more than the hard facts about the deceased such as names, etc. Also the important messages of love, feelings and emotions are

communicated through clairsentience. In the example of Martin Cooper's communication he was able to impress me with clairsentience to show that he had damaged his head, had arthritis in his right hand and had a stomach condition. The emotional feelings expressed for his mother also came through clairsentience.

CLAIRVOYANCE

You will understand by now that just as feelings can be communicated by telepathy so can pictures. Mediums refer to clairvoyance as the mental pictures they are shown by a spirit communicator that appear in their third eye chakra. The images 'seen' can include the deceased's facial features, the house where they lived, scenes from their life or important objects that are significant proofs of identity. The example quoted shows how Martin Cooper gave visual information such as the doorway where he died, the matted hair of his poodle dog and the broken watch, all shown to me in the form of a picture. Good clairvoyance can give excellent proof that the person you once knew and loved hasn't sunk into oblivion but lives again in a new and better world.

CLAIRAUDIENCE

This is when the telepathic communication from the spirit communicator is 'heard' by the medium as a voice. This is a mental blending of the medium's thoughts with the spirit communicator and is sometimes experienced as an audible voice, but usually as an inner one. Often we can give the name and surname of the spirit communicator, the number and street where they used to live, their birth date and passing date and unlimited information, facts and advice to guide the sitter or relieve their grief. In Martin Cooper's case he was able to give me his full name as well as names of places and people.

Mediumship is therefore a form of telepathic communication with people from the afterlife. It combines psychic sensing, seeing and hearing. The examples I have given relate to what is known as 'mental mediumship' but spirit communication can take other forms as well:

Inspirational   The medium talks on a chosen subject and feels his words and train of thought influenced by spirit people.

Mental   The medium senses, sees and hears the spirit communicator and passes on the information he is given.

Trance   The spirit communicator talks directly through the medium's voice.

Physical   An entranced medium, sitting in a pitch-dark room, exudes a white luminous substance called ectoplasm. This misty substance solidifies into the form of spirit people known by the seance members. Sometimes a rod of ectoplasm is formed that enables a spirit to talk through a trumpet.

Transfiguration   Ectoplasm forms only over the entranced medium's face. The superimposed face of the spirit communicator is seen by the participants.

Direct voice   Mediums like Leslie Flint evolved an artificial voice box created out of ectoplasm. The spirit voice is disembodied and can be heard from different parts of the room.

Proof of the afterlife

Many great names throughout history have been convinced that mediumistic communication with the afterlife is possible. These include Sir Arthur Conan Doyle, William Crooks, Madam Curie, Lord Downing, Thomas Edison and Queen Victoria. Some of the most important studies of mediumistic communication have been undertaken by the Society for Psychical Research (SPR). When its founders Frederick W. Myres, Henry Sidgewick and Edmund Gurney died, a group of unconnected mediums living in England, America and India started receiving messages from them. The resulting transcripts became known as the Cross Correspondence. The SPR spirit communicators, who had while living studied the classics, relayed a fragmented series of cryptic conundrums that only made sense when they were collected together four years later. Their communications alluded to obscure Greek history relating to the afterlife myths and the tombs of Alexander, Lorenzo de Medici and Giuliano – references only an advanced scholar of the classics

would understand. There can be no question of telepathy since the mediums themselves did not understand the clues.

Deathbed visions have provided a rich source of material to suggest that an afterlife exists. The philosopher Emanuel Swedenborg, arguably the first modern medium, predicted the exact date of his death weeks in advance. A servant girl who was present at his passing said, 'He was pleased, as if he was going to have a holiday, to go on some merry-making.'

Similarly, the poet and artist William Blake, had ecstatic visions as he lay dying. His friends, who sat with him, said that Blake stared into space and drew pictures of spirit people that he saw clearly. His wife wrote: 'Just before he died his countenance became fair – his eyes brightened, and he burst out in singing of the things he saw in heaven.'

William Wordsworth, at the point of his death, saw his dead sister Dorothy come for him. And the Duke of Windsor, whose life was wrecked when he married divorcee Wallis Simpson, saw in his deathbed vision on 22 May 1972 his deceased mother Queen Mary come for him. Had his mother forgiven him in death for all those things she could never forgive in life?

Modern research into the survival of death is today being undertaken by many doctors and surgeons who are collecting testimonials from patients who have come close to death. These Near Death Experiences (NDEs) have proved remarkably consistent.

Although clinically brain-dead during surgery the resuscitated patients have described vivid experiences of leaving their bodies and entering the afterlife. Many have been free of drugs and without religious preconceptions. Their experiences have been fully lucid and unlike a dream can be remembered in vivid detail which suggests that these reports are not induced by the anaesthetic or a result of opium-like chemicals released by the brain during stress.

Some of the most interesting reports collected have been from children. Dr Kubler-Ross made extensive studies of NDE patients involved in multiple-death family car accidents. She quotes many

instances where dying children have known which family members have died and have given the correct circumstances and times of their passing.

Other cases studied are of adults who claim to have left their body during surgery and have seen the events taking place in the operating theatre. Dr Michael Sabom quotes the experience of a US Air Force pilot who, after being resuscitated from a massive heart-attack, described an out-of-body experience where he correctly saw the numbers displayed on the defibrillator display even though it was completely out of his line of sight.

One blind patient described in minute detail the designs and colours of the clothing being worn by her surgeons. Another blind patient was able to give the numbers registered on the anaesthetist's machinery. And in perhaps the most famous NDE case a woman travelling out of her body during an operation reported that she saw a battered gym shoe with a hole in its toe lodged high up on one of the hospital's windowsills. The shoe was later found to be exactly where she said and could not have been seen prior to its discovery.

Subjects from a wide cultural mix and differing religious beliefs who have undergone a Near Death Experience describe an afterlife that is very real. After the initial out-of-body experience they describe a tunnel of light that draws them into a beautiful ethereal place where they encounter their dead loved ones. It is the same world that mystics, prophets, visionaries and mediums have been describing for centuries.

Many people marvel at mediumship but by now you will understand that it is built upon the simple psychic faculties that many ordinary people have. You may not yet be able to give a clear and precise message from the spirit world but you will see in your own spontaneous ESP experiences a framework upon which you can build towards a communication with the afterlife.

The power behind psychic phenomena

Mystics say that matter is materialised mind-stuff, and some of them like Jesus or Sai Baba today, have proved this by demonstrating the power to materialise and dematerialise their bodies or physical objects. There is an inexhaustible energy all around us. In the East they call this energy *prana* and theoretical physicists here in the West are proposing a similar inexhaustible universal force called zero point energy. From this great ocean of conscious spiritual energy comes all form. The Absolute vibrates at differing frequencies to manifest as light, sound, electricity, matter and most importantly as the life-force and consciousness.

Yogis teach us that consciousness, mind, body and matter are manifestations of the one energy which is essentially mental in nature. Everything is essentially the same energy vibrating at different rates. Prana is a universal principle which pervades all space and in its highest form manifests as the life-force. Every living organism absorbs it and it is by this pranic force that all activity is carried on in the body from thinking to bodily movements.

We are all channels for this cosmic energy. If we are enthusiastic about the work we do, we are revitalised by its power. Alternatively, if we fight against the cosmic tide by working at something that we detest we often become depleted and stagnant. When we are ill we can draw this power into ourselves as a healing force or may channel it through ourselves to heal others. And just as we draw in these powers so we also radiate them. We are all spiritual transmitters pouring the vibrations of our consciousness into the world around us. These powers communicate to the unconscious of others and can even influence our fortunes.

Transferring psychic energy (prana)

Most people who develop their psychic or mediumistic gifts discover that they have a natural healing potential as well. The reason being that they have stimulated and expanded their auric body. Instead of being a hardened shell the auric light is now more ready to absorb and channel the pranic energies directly from the cosmos. Consequently many start on a path that they believe to be of a psychic nature but are drawn toward the healing arts as they progress. The great healer Harry Edwards, for example, began his life as a very gifted medium but went on to become one of the most famous spiritual healers of all time. Psychic and healing powers draw on the same pranic energy that flows through the sensitised and open aura.

They say that everyone with sincere intent can heal. Many people heal unconsciously. The touch of a doctor, nurse, care assistant or parent will often bring relief without them having the faintest idea how they are doing this. These people are easy to recognise as you will feel calm and restored in their presence. If we hurt ourselves we spontaneously put our hands on the affected part, a mother does the same for her children, and if we have a headache we instinctively rub our brow with our hands. Healing is so simple that it scarcely needs to be taught.

The healing prana energy is influenced by and directed by thought. Yogis advise that we can increase our own vitality by visualising the prana energy as a bright light being drawn in through the breath that then spreads throughout the body. Many yogis do not practise the laying on of hands to transfer the prana. It can be projected from the eye through gazing or by the projection of thought during meditation. Methods such as Reiki healing employ the use of inwardly visualised symbols to increase the mental bond between healer and patient.

The principle of psychic healing rests on the fact that prana may be transferred from one person to another. The traditional and probably most effective method is to use the hands and make passes over the sick person. A prana current, that can be seen by those visually

aware of the aura, flows through the hands to the affected part. The patient's aura is stimulated which in turn activates the sluggish cell-groups. In this way energy is transferred to the patient, who becomes invigorated, strengthened and in time healed. The power is not taken from the healer's own aura but should be seen as flowing through him and drawn from the infinite cosmic source. Many healers are aware that spiritual helpers are with them who help to guide and direct the energy. It is not necessary to be aware of these spirit guides but it helps to be aware that the healing powers are not your own but given to you from a higher dimension. If you try healing for yourself and begin feeling drained then stop or you will deplete your own prana reserves that are stored in your body.

The healing energy will flow more vigorously if the healer's breath is slow and rhythmical and his mind focused on projecting loving positive thoughts towards his patient. The thoughts that the healer projects should not be anxious about the illness or the effectiveness of his powers. Instead the mind should imagine that the patient is happy and well and that the healing energy is gently doing its work. Some yogic techniques suggest that we inwardly talk to the affected part of the body encouraging it as we would a small child who needs to be coaxed towards better behaviour. A gentle but firm command is intermingled with the loving kindness that projects from you. In this way the healing light enters the patient.

how to heal

Techniques differ between the various healing schools and there are no hard and fast rules. Many healers will hold their hands in a still position and allow the prana energy to flow from them. Usually they start at the patient's head and systematically work downward towards their feet. Sometimes the healer's intuition will impress them to work for a longer period on one particular area where they feel a cold spot. It may not be the area where the patient has the complaint, but areas where you feel an overtly hot or cold sensation in the hands are normally those where there is a blockage in the patient's auric body. Unblock this area and the patient's own prana will flow more freely, enabling their life-forces to become balanced.

In most cases the healers do not touch the patient and hold their hands a few inches from the body. (This is particularly important for male healers to bear in mind to avoid any potential malpractice accusations of a sexual nature.) Yogic methods claim that the speed of movement of the hands relates to the nature of the pranic energy transmitted. For example a slow, gentle passing of the hands brings a calming energy, whereas a quick passing has a stimulating effect. Some methods employ a twisting movement of the fingers about six inches away from the body as if boring holes in it. This will spiral energy to specific areas that may be congested or sluggish. The best advice is to go with what your own intuition tells you. Every healer adopts their own favourite motions which come to them instinctively.

a healing session

An environment that is restful is conducive a good results, so perhaps you could play a little gentle music, put some flowers in the room and light an aromatic oil burner. Sit your patient in a comfortable chair and reassure them that healing can help them. Explain that they may feel a gentle heat and sometimes a coolness coming from your hands. Don't make exaggerated claims or advise them to discontinue their doctor's instructions of course. All they have to do is close their eyes and remain relaxed and receptive. They don't have to believe in what you do or change their religious convictions. No faith is required.

Hold the hands apart with the fingers extended and separated. Raise your hands above your patient's head and visualise the healing energy as a brilliant white light flowing from your fingertips. Sense that your patient's aura is opening to receive the healing energy. Most healers start with the head so that the healing energy relaxes the patient. Once they relax you will become aware of the pranic flow increasing. Continue until you feel that your patient is ready and then move your hands away in a downward sweeping motion and gently swing the fingers sideways as if you were flicking water from them. Do this every time you finish working on a fixed area or make a sweeping pass with the hands. Close the fingers as you do this then open them again as you begin healing the next area.

Most healers systematically work downwards, healing the shoulders, back, stomach, etc. then do the same at the front of the person, working gradually to the feet. If you sense a cold area in the patient's aura focus on this part for a little longer. Remember to visualise the light flowing from your fingers and bathing the patient, and reinforce this with positive mental thoughts of love and health. After healing each area, flick the fingers as before. During the session you will probably want to move your hands with the energy flow. Let your intuition guide you. Work on the areas you feel most drawn to and pass the hands in downward, gentle, sweeping movements wherever you feel inclined. Some healers like to make sweeping movements to the whole body from the head and downwards to the feet.

When you feel the energy subside it is time to stop; the work has been done. Now place your hands above the patient's head and imagine that their aura is closing. Your telepathic commands will do this. Finally let the patient remain still and quiet until they feel fully restored. You may perhaps suggest that they sit in an armchair if one is available. And don't be surprised if they fall asleep!

6

CONNECTING

Throughout this book I have endeavoured to demystify psychic phenomena and tried to demonstrate that ESP talents are within everyone's grasp. You now have a basic understanding of the main aspects of psychic skills. You will understand what telepathy, clairvoyance, precognition and psychokinesis are and may have learnt a little about developing your potential for mediumship and healing. You know how to recognise psychic powers in others and no doubt some of the psychic skills I've outlined you've already experienced yourself. Many people today are experiencing a silent spiritual transformation as their latent psychic powers begin to flower.

In time the gifts of second sight will be accepted as normal, and spiritual powers will be treasured by future generations. This is a dangerous yet exciting age in which to be born, as these mighty forces of spirituality and love begin to awaken in the hearts of men. In the future our present civilisation will seem like a Dark Age and the materialism that we so willingly embrace will seem like a barbaric anachronism. Quality of life will be more important than material prosperity, with competition replaced by co-operation; surgery may be replaced by a scientific understanding of healing powers and the afterlife will freely communicate with this world to share its ageless wisdom. Or as the teacher Sai Baba tells us, 'Truth and virtue will triumph, character rather than wealth will confer power, and wisdom will be enthroned in the councils of nations.'

You are taking the first steps on a spiritual road. Be encouraged for many will soon join you.

Psychic and spiritual unfoldment

Today we are seeing the decline of traditional religion and the birth of a 'new' spirituality based upon self-discovery and direct experience. No longer are people prepared to accept the bigoted opinions of religious leaders or priests as the only version of truth. People want to test the truth for themselves and find spirituality through direct experience. Science has taught us to question nature, and modern spiritual thinking inspires us towards self-inquiry and to question the superficial reality of the world that we once took for granted. As a consequence many spiritual seekers reject literal orthodoxy and embrace what the philosophers call the *philosophia perennis* – the eternal truths that forever reappear throughout history. The inner spiritual potential of our species is beginning to awaken.

The emergence of psychic powers is only one small step up the spiritual ladder. The result of spiritual development should be to inspire the aspirant to heal the sick, uplift the broken hearted and, most importantly, to improve their own behaviour and morality. If you work hard to advance your ESP skills it may appear that the powers you have developed are your own but you will realise as you progress that you are really only a channel for psychic or healing powers. They are not yours to possess and should be used in service to the highest. The goal of meditation and self-control, that awakens psychic powers, should be compassion.

The egotistical pitfall

A subtle spiritual egotism can sometimes overtake even those who apparently lead dedicated lives and it takes a great deal of self-examination and personal honesty to discover it. There is nothing more sickening than the self-righteous psychic who indulges in the praise and honour that psychic powers can bring. Some of the greatest mediums and psychics had tremendous powers but displayed personalities as despicable as the most blatant materialist. In short,

for psychic powers to flower properly they must be developed together with high moral and spiritual values. Know that you are doing service and remain humble within.

Humour can be the best medicine for the expansive ego. Place me in front of an audience and I will boast of my psychic abilities and praise myself to the point that the audience know that I am being silly. I will tell them what a wonderfully modest person I am. In this way I laugh at my self-importance yet, hopefully, remain humble within. In other words, don't take yourself or your powers too seriously. Egotism is our first and last enemy. If you decide that you need a psychic or spiritual teacher make sure that they too know how to laugh at themselves.

Connecting to your inner teachers

The process of spiritual transformation and the triggering of psychic powers is a slow and continuous process but you may find that at certain points in your life the spiritual soil is fertile enough for rapid advancement to take place. By reading books like this one, you are planting the seeds of future development. Perhaps some tragedy or period of adversity has stimulated you to question your life and to seek out new ways of dealing with your situation. At first you may progress alone but inevitably you will meet others who are on the same path as yourself. Like the travellers in Herman Hess's novel *Journey to the East*, we miraculously encounter fellow spiritual travellers when we are ready for knowledge. Somehow the Fates conspire to bring us together with other seekers.

Listed at the end of this book are a number of large organisations which may help you with your search for fellow seekers. However, there are also many small informal psychic groups all over the world that are not affiliated with any organisation, and these may offer exactly what you need spiritually. When you start changing the way you think and perceive the world, the influences upon your

circumstances start changing as well. Sometimes it will feel as if you are being drawn down a river of remarkable coincidences that are leading you to the great sea of universal truth. Trust your inner voice and go with the flow. Alternatively, why not start your own group from the seekers you will encounter and invite different psychics and lecturers each week to teach you?

To work with others quickens your psychic and spiritual development, awakens new ideas and reinforces what you are trying to accomplish.

Unseen influences

As you sincerely try to enhance your psychic abilities by persistent practice alone or in a group, you will almost certainly become aware of help being given to you from the 'higher' spiritual planes. As you increase your own level of awareness the discarnate spiritual beings become aware of your earnest intention to progress and you may gradually sense them taking an interest in you. If your motives are pure these guides and teachers will aid you with your work during sleep, meditation or when you are practising psychic skills. They come on a vibration of love, so there's nothing to be afraid of. Also they will reveal themselves only gradually to you and at a time when you are spiritually ready. They work at your own pace and it may take a very long time before you know them fully.

In my own case the spirit guides have drawn close over many years, and my trust in them is so complete that I allow them to speak through me when I am in trance. This started at first as a blending of thoughts which has developed now into a form where I am unconscious of what is being spoken through me. Trance mediumship should, in my opinion, only be developed at a later stage and only after the medium can accomplish accurate mental mediumship. There are many crackpots who claim to be trance mediums but whose 'guides' can never give proof of their reality. My own spiritual teacher will allow many spirit people to speak through me who were well known to the people who sit with me. They provide evidence of survival that bears testimony to the reality of the trance channel.

Talk to your angel

The word angel in Greek means 'messenger', and since ancient times these celestial beings have inspired and comforted mankind from the realm beyond the earth. Archaeologists have traced a belief in angels to as far back as 2500 BC where we hear of an angel to Babylon and even earlier references are found in the Egyptian pantheon and the carvings of Mesopotamia and Assyria. The angels in the Old Testament were not winged beings but companions and teachers that descended from heaven. The angel that visited Abraham was an ordinary human being and Jacob's angels climbed down a ladder. In India the yogi who has no earthly guru may receive his instruction from a guru in the spirit.

Angels can still be our companions, messengers and teachers. Some may never have taken earthly form and others may be advanced souls who walked the earth centuries ago. Many people, such as my wife Jane for example, are guided and taught by deceased relatives and friends who have passed into the spirit realm. But it does not matter whether your spiritual helper was a saint, a king, a peasant or a philosopher, it is the message that they bring that is of importance. It is wise to remember that it is often the humblest people who lead the most spiritual lives.

During your meditations you may also glimpse the spirit form of someone who has known and loved you, such as a wife, husband, father, mother or grandparent. Open yourself to these influences and you will feel great happiness and security. As they develop their telepathic bond and you trust the reality of their presence they will gradually be able to give you spiritual and material guidance. But don't expect everything all at once. You may not 'see' them but sense them. You may feel the atmosphere of their presence or feel their personality. You will remember how I taught you that clairsentience is the foundation upon which clairvoyant vision and clairaudient communication are built?

At first you may sense and then begin to inwardly see lights, visions or hear their gentle voice. In the silence of meditation they will

slowly be able to impress you and finally guide you. Your ethereal hosts impart a silent influence and will blend, if you wish it, their thoughts with your own.

Do not bombard them with impatient questions and requests. Keep your communications simple and the clarity of their answer will become apparent. Their reply may not come immediately but only at a time when you are spiritually ready to receive their answer. Sometimes their answers may come as an intuitive impression to read a certain book or see another person who will give you the guidance you need. Alternatively, they may flood you with a feeling of great peace, happiness, healing or well-being that may be just the spiritual medicine you need at that moment. Finally, you will see their face in your mind's eye and clairaudiently hear their voice.

Are the angels real?

The Swiss analytical psychologist Carl Jung believed that his spiritual life was guided by a higher being who he named Philemon and who first appeared to him in a dream. 'Philemon represented a force which was not myself,' wrote Carl Jung. 'In my fantasies I held conversations with him, and he said things which I had not consciously thought. For I observed clearly that it was he who spoke, not I.' This lame, winged priest from the pagan traditions Jung assumed was a symbolic representation of superior insight. In effect it was his own inner guru or teacher. However, he observed that the figure seemed to be separate from himself. 'At times he seemed to me quite real, as if he were a living personality.'

Whether the spiritual guides and angels are aspects of ourselves, yet to be integrated into the personality, or independent beings will always be a subject of debate. Carl Jung was not particularly impressed by the claims of the Spiritualist mediums who he briefly studied. I believe, however, that the spiritual teachers are real beings, but perhaps the question is unimportant as both will lead you to higher knowledge. The important thing to do is to listen to the gentle voice within and decide for yourself.

CONNECTING WITH PSYCHICS, MEDIUMS AND HEALERS

The following advice and listings should give you a few pointers to help you find a psychic, healer or teaching organisation. If you write to any of the following contacts please remember to enclose a stamped, self-addressed envelope. Many spiritually oriented organisations work on a financial shoe string.

PSYCHIC CONSULTATIONS

As with every profession there are good and bad practitioners. There are hundreds of thousands of psychics working throughout the world, and yet only a handful may have a true psychic gift. I have never met an outright fraudster but there are many psychics working today who are frankly not good enough to be charging a fee. Unfortunately there is no internationally recognised register of psychics and many display certificates, etc. that are not worth the paper they're printed on.

The best psychics and mediums rarely need to advertise as their sitters come to them through personal recommendation. So the most effective way to find a genuine practitioner is to ask people you know. Also, many cities now have 'New Age' shops where many psychics display their literature. Ask the proprietor if they know of someone with a good reputation.

MEDIUMISTIC CONSULTATIONS

Many, but not all, good mediums are monitored by Spiritualists. Their weekly newspaper *Psychic News* has a classified section for mediums and a 'New Age' section for psychics, etc. Before accepting an advertisement the editor insists that verifiable testimonials from sitters or Spiritualist Churches are supplied. Although they wouldn't claim their method to be totally failsafe you do, however, stand a better chance of seeing someone genuine. The newspaper also contains information about Spiritualist Churches and events in the UK, America, Canada, South Africa, Australia and New Zealand.

Psychic News

Can be ordered in the UK through your newsagent or write direct to: Psychic News, Clock Cottage, Stansted Hall, Mountfitchet, Essex CM24 8UD, UK. Tel: 01279 817050

Other organisations that check their practitioners and may be able to put you in touch with a psychic or medium in your area include:

The Spiritualist Association of Great Britain (SAGB)

Visiting mediums give public demonstrations to an audience and resident mediums can be booked for consultations.

The Spiritualist Association of Great Britain, 33 Belgrave Square, London SW1X 8QB, UK.

Similar organisations overseas include:

The Australian Spiritual Association

PO Box 273, Penrith, NSW 2747, Australia. Tel: (07) 8496450

The Spiritualist Church of Canada

1835 Lawrence Ave. E. Scarborough, Ontario, Canada, M1R 2Y3. Tel: (416) 439-1087

Societies and Colleges

The following organisations will be able to recommend a psychic or medium and offer training for those who want to learn:

The College of Psychic Studies

16 Queensberry Place, London, SW7 2EB.

The Institute of Spiritualist Mediums

20 Oakhurst Ave, East Barnet, Hertfordshire, EN4 8DL, UK.

CONSULTATIONS WITH THE AUTHOR

My wife and I give psychic and mediumistic consultations from our home, and run development groups and occasionally tour England and abroad:

Craig Hamilton-Parker: 23 Mitre Copse, Bishopstoke, Eastleigh, Hampshire, SO50 8QE, UK. Tel: (01703) 696262

PSYCHIC FAIRS

Many psychics and fortune tellers work at psychic fairs, and Jane and I have organised many of these ourselves. Unfortunately most organisers are only interested in commercial considerations and will rent their tables to anyone without checking if the practitioners are experienced or reputable. The annual *Festivals of Mind, Body and Spirit* are discerning about who they choose and offer an excellent platform for a wide spectrum of spiritually oriented exhibitors. Festivals take place in London, England, America and Australia. To be put on their mailing list write to: New Life Promotions Limited, Arnica House, 170 Campden Hill Road, London, W8 7AS, UK. Tel: 0171- 938 3788

TELEPHONE READINGS

A report in the USA in 1996 revealed an estimated $100 million a year is spent on the various commercial 'Dial a psychic' lines that you may see advertised in your daily paper. A report from Australia claimed that psychics at the end of a phone simply turned to a manual of messages and answers to questions to advise callers. It is possible to give a proper consultation over the phone but make sure you are calling an individual practitioner and are not being charged excessive phone rates.

CONNECTING WITH TRAINING ORGANISATIONS

The Internet is a global network that links the computers of the world together. You can connect through a modem that links your home computer through your telephone line or visit one of the many 'Cyber Cafes' that are opening all over the world. For a massive list of psychic, paranormal and spiritual organisations simply log in to the net. Alternatively, you could write to the following organisations to find out what psychic, mediumistic or spiritual training courses are available:

The Arthur Findlay College
This world famous college offers residential courses for Spiritual and Psychic investigation and instruction. It offers special courses in a range of foreign languages. The Arthur Findlay College, Stansted Hall, Stansted Mountfitchet, Essex, CM24 8UD, UK.

The Swedenborg Movement
Promotes the teachings of the Swedish philosopher and medium Emanuel Swedenborg. Their residential centre at Purley Chase offers courses in spiritual development and awareness. They will send you a free magazine called *Outlook*. The Swedenborg Movement, 98 Abbotts Drive, Wembley, Middlesex, HA0 3SQ, UK.

The British Astrological and Psychic Society
Provides a national register of consultants, basic astrological courses and workshops. The British Astrological and Psychic Society, 124 Trefoil Crescent, Broadfield, West Sussex, RH11 9EZ, UK.

The Anthroposophical Society
Spiritual teachings and weekend workshops based on the philosophy of Rudolf Steiner. The Anthroposophical Society, 35 Park Road, London, NW1 6XT, UK.

Gaunt House
A varied programme of workshops to promote and nurture self-realisation. Gaunts House, Wimborne, Dorset, BH21 4JQ, UK.

The White Eagle Lodge
A spiritual organisation based on trance teachings from the spirit guide calling himself White Eagle. The White Eagle Lodge, New Lands, Brewells Lane, Liss, Hampshire, GU33 7HY, UK.

Planetary Connections
To find out about the New Age movement around the world and get to know of individuals and organisations that are active in your area or country subscribe to this excellent newspaper. It is available free in New Age shops or can be posted to you for a small donation. Planetary Connection, The Six Bells, Church Street, Bishops Castle, Shropshire, SY9 5AA, UK.

Connecting with Healing

Healing, absent healing, and training are available from the following organisations.

National Federation of Spiritual Healers
This organisation will recommend a good healer who practises in your area and offers training opportunities and a code of conduct for those who want to learn to heal. The National Federation of Spiritual Healers, Old Manor Farm Studio, Church Street, Sudbury-on-Thames, Middlesex, TW16 6RG, UK.

The Harry Edwards Spiritual Healing Sanctuary
Based on the wonderful powers and teachings of Harry Edwards this sincere organisation offers healing, absent healing and instruction. The Harry Edwards Spiritual Healing Sanctuary Trust, Burrows Lea, Shere, Guildford, Surrey, GU5 9QG, UK,

Connecting with the East

The great spiritual teachings continue to flow from Mother India. There are many teachers who may be able to help you on your spiritual path and who display miraculous powers. I suggest that the reader consider the philosophy of the following great gurus:

Sathya Sai Baba

Sai Baba's ashram in India attracts thousands of followers. It is almost impossible to get close to this great teacher. However, to link up with the movement and practise its spiritual methods you need only to harmonise with the vibrations of love that unite his followers. If you'd like some information about Sai Baba groups in your area or would like to see the ashram write to: Sathya Sai Baba Information Centre, PO Box 7722, San Diego, California, 92107 USA.

The Self-Realisation Fellowship

The Kriya Yoga techniques of Paramahansa Yogananda offer practical methods toward self-realisation. For details write to: Self-Realisation Fellowship, 3880 San Rafael Avenue, Los Angeles, California, 90065, USA.

CONNECTING WITH BOOKS

Books should be more than a method of obtaining knowledge. They should encourage us to change our lives and turn knowledge into wisdom. Some of the books that have inspired this one and that have fuelled my own spiritual quest include:

Alpert, Richard, (RAM DASS) *Journey of Awakening*, Bantam Books, Toronto, 1978.

Barrett, Sir William, *On the Threshold of the Unseen*, Kegan Paul, Trench Trubner & Co., London, 1920.

Blavatsky, Helen Petrovna, *The Voice of the Silence*, Theosophical Publishing House, India.

Borgia, Anthony, *Life in the World Unseen*, Odhams Press Ltd., London.

Douglas, Alfred, *Extra Sensory Powers*, Victor Gollancz Ltd., London, 1976.

Doyle, Sir Arthur Conan, *The New Revelation and the Vital Message*, Psychic Press Ltd., London, 1981.

Dunne, J. W. *An Experiment with Time*, Macmillan, London, 1981.

Edwards, Harry, *A Guide for the Development of Mediumship*, Psychic Press Ltd., London, 1976.

Eysenck, Hans J. and Sergent, Carl, *Explaining the Unexplained*, Book Club Associates, London, 1982.

Findlay, Arthur, *The Rock of Truth*, Psychic Press, London, 1933.

Fortune, Dion, *Psychic Self-Defence*, Samuel Weiser Inc., New York, 1930.

Greaves, Helen, *Testimony of Light*, Neville Spearman Ltd., Suffolk, 1969.

Gurney, E., Myres, F. W. H. and Podmore, Frank, *Phantasms of the Living. Volume I and II*, Trubner & Co., London, 1886.

Hamilton-Parker, Craig, *The Psychic Workbook*, Vermilion, Random House, London, 1995.

Hess, Herman, *The Journey to the East*, Noonday, New York, 1965.

Higginson, Gordon, *On the side of Angels*, Tudor Press, London, 1993.

Hislop, John Dr, *My Baba and I*, Birth Day Publishing Co., San Diego, California, 1985.

Huxley, Aldous, *Perennial Philosophy*, Harper Colophon, New York, 1945.

Jung, C. G. *Memories, Dreams, Reflections*, Collins and Routledge & Kegan Paul, London, 1963.

Lodge, Sir Oliver, *Raymond or Life and Death*, Methuen & Co. Ltd, London, 1916.

Manning, Matthew, *The Link*, Colin Smythe Ltd., Bucks, 1974.

Mitchell, Edgar D. *Psychic Exploration*, G.P. Putnam & Sons, New York, 1974.

Monroe, Robert A. *Journeys out of the Body*, Souvenir Press Ltd., London, 1972.

Moody, Raymond A. *Life After Life*, Bantam Books, New York, 1975.

Murphet, Howard, *Sai Baba Avatar*, Macmillan India Ltd., Madras, 1978.

Northage, Ivy, *The Mechanics of Mediumship*, Graphic Colour Print, Emsworth, 1973.

Ornstein, Robert, E. *The Psychology of Consciousness*, Penguin, London, 1972.

Ostrander, Sheila and Schroeder, Lynn, *PSI Psychic Discoveries behind the Iron Curtain*, Sphere Books Ltd., London, 1973.

Ouspensky, P. D. *A New Model of the Universe*, Routledge & Kegan Paul, London, 1931.

Owen, Iris M. and Sparrow, Margaret, *Conjuring up Philip*, Fitzhenry & Whiteside, Ontario, Canada, 1976.

Owen, Robert Dale, *The Debatable Land between this World and the Next*, Trubner & Co., London, 1874.

Puharich, Andrija, *Beyond Telepathy*, Doubleday & Co Inc., New York, 1962.

Ramacharaka, Yogi, *The Science of Psychic Healing*, L.N. Fowler & Co Ltd., London, 1960.

Rhine, Joseph B. *New Frontiers of the Mind*, Pelican Books, London, 1937.

Richet, Charles, Ph.D. *Thirty Years of Psychical Research*, W. Collins Sons & Co Ltd., London, 1923.

Steiner, Rudolf, Ph.D, *An Outline of Occult Science*, Theosophical Publishing Society, London, 1914.

Stokes, Doris, *Voices in my ear*, Macdonald & Co Ltd., London, 1979.

Storm, Stella, *Philosophy of Silver Birch*, Psychic Press, London, 1969.

Swann, Ingo, *To Kiss Earth Goodbye*, Hawthorn Books Inc. New York, 1975.

Swedenborg, Emmanuel, *Swedenborg's Works*, Houghton Mifflin, New York.

Tart, Charles T. *Altered States of Consciousness*, Doubleday & Co. Inc., New York, 1969.

Taylor, Professor John, *Superminds*, Macmillan, London, 1975.

Tester, M. H. *Learning to Live*, Psychic Press, London, 1983.

Tompkins, Peter and Bird, Christopher, *The Secret Life of Plants*, Harper & Row, London, 1973.

Trine, Ralph Waldo, *In Tune with the Infinite*, Harper Collins, London, 1899.

Waite, A. E. *The Pictorial Key to the Tarot*, Random House, London, 1910.

Watkins, Alfred, *The Old Straight Track*, Garnstone Press, London, 1970.

Watson, Lyall, *Supernature*, Hodder & Stroughton, London, 1973.

Wilhelm, Richard, *The I Ching*, Routledge & Kegan Paul, London, 1951.

Wilson, Colin, *Mysteries*, Hodder & Stoughton, London, 1978.

Wilson, Ian, *The After Death Experience*, Bantam Books, London, 1987.

Woodroffe, Sir John, *The Serpent Power*, Ganesh & Co., Madras-17, India, 1974.

Yogananda, Paramahansa, *Autobiography of a Yogi*, Self-Realisation Fellowship, Los Angeles, California, 1959.

Other titles in this series

Astral Projection 0 340 67418 0   Is it possible for the soul to leave the body at will? In this book the traditional techniques used to achieve astral projection are described in a simple, practical way, and Out of the Body and Near Death Experiences are also explored.

Chakras 0 340 62082 X   The body's energy centres, the chakras, can act as gateways to healing and increased self-knowledge. This book shows you how to work with chakras in safety and with confidence.

Chinese Horoscopes 0 340 64804 X   In the Chinese system of horoscopes, the year of birth is all-important. *Chinese Horoscopes for beginners* tells you how to determine your own Chinese horoscope, what personality traits you are likely to have, and how your fortunes may fluctuate in years to come.

Dowsing 0 340 60882 X   People all over the world have used dowsing since the earliest times. This book shows how to start dowsing – what to use, what to dowse, and what to expect when subtle energies are detected.

Dream Interpretation 0 340 60150 7   This fascinating introduction to the art and science of dream interpretation explains how to unravel the meaning behind dream images to interpret your own and other people's dreams.

Feng Shui 0 340 62079 X   This beginner's guide to the ancient art of luck management will show you how to increase your good fortune and well-being by harmonising your environment with the natural energies of the earth.

Gems and Crystals 0 340 60883 8   For centuries gems and crystals have been used as an aid to healing and meditation. This guide tells you all you need to know about choosing, keeping and using stones to increase your personal awareness and improve your well-being.

Graphology 0 340 60625 8   Graphology, the science of interpreting handwriting to reveal personality, is now widely accepted and used throughout the world. This introduction will enable you to make a comprehensive analysis of your own and other people's handwriting to reveal the hidden self.

Herbs for magic and ritual 0 340 67415 6   This book looks at the well-known herbs and the stories attached to them. There is essential information on the use of herbs in essential oils and incense, and on their healing and magical qualities.

I Ching 0 340 62080 3   The roots of *I Ching* or the *Book of Changes* lie in the time of the feudal mandarin lords of China, but its traditional wisdom is still relevant today. Using the original poetry in its translated form, this introduction traces its history, survival and modern-day applications.

Love Signs 0 340 64805 8   This is a practical introduction to the astrology of romantic relationships. It explains the different roles played by each of the planets, focusing particularly on the position of the Moon at the time of birth.

Meditation 0 340 64835 X   This beginner's guide gives simple, clear instructions to enable you to start meditating and benefiting from this ancient mental discipline immediately. The text is illustrated throughout by full-colour photographs and line drawings.

Numerology 0 340 59551 5   Despite being scientifically based, numerology requires no great mathematical talents to understand. This introduction gives you all the information you will need to understand the significance of numbers in your everyday life.

Paganism 0 340 67013 4   Pagans are true Nature worshippers who celebrate the cycles of life. This guide describes pagan festivals and rituals and takes a detailed look at the many forms of paganism practised today.

Palmistry 0 340 59552 3   Palmistry is the oldest form of character reading still in use. This illustrated guide shows you exactly what to look for and how to interpret what you find.

Qabalah 0 340 67339 7   The Qabalah is an ancient Jewish system of spiritual knowledge centred on the Tree of Life. This guide explains how it can be used in meditation and visualisation, and links it to the chakras, yoga, colour therapy, crystals, Tarot and numerology.

Runes 0 340 62081 1   The power of the runes in healing and giving advice about relationships and life in general has been acknowledged since the time of the Vikings. This book shows how runes can be used in our technological age to increase personal awareness and stimulate individual growth.

Spiritual Healing 0 340 67416 4   All healing starts with self, and the Universal Power which makes this possible is available to everyone. In this book there are exercises, techniques and guidelines to follow which will enable you to heal yourself and others spiritually.

Star Signs 0 340 59553 1   This detailed analysis looks at each of the star signs in turn and reveals how your star sign affects everything about you. This book shows you how to use this knowledge in your relationships and in everyday life.

Tarot 0 340 59550 7   Tarot cards have been used for many centuries. This guide gives advice on which sort to buy, where to get them and how to use them. The emphasis is on using the cards positively, as a tool for gaining self-knowledge, while exploring present and future possibilities.

The Moon and You 0 340 64836 8   The phase of the Moon when you were born radically affects your personality. This book looks at nine lunar types – how they live, love, work and play, and provides simple tables to find out the phase of your birth.

Visualisation 0 340 65495 3   This introduction to visualisation, a form of self-hypnosis widely used by Buddhists, will show you how to practise the basic techniques – to relieve stress, improve your health and increase your sense of personal well-being.

Witchcraft 0 340 67014 2   This guide to the ancient religion based on Nature worship answers many of the questions and uncovers the myths and misconceptions surrounding witchcraft. Mystical rituals and magic are explained and there is advice for the beginner on how to celebrate the Sabbats.

Your Psychic Powers 0 340 67417 2   Are you psychic? This book will help you find out by encouraging you to look more deeply within yourself. Psychic phenomena such as precognitive dreams, out of body travels and visits from the dead are also discussed in this ideal stepping stone towards a more aware you.

To order this series

All books in this series are available from bookshops or, in case of difficulty, can be ordered direct from the publisher. Just fill in the form below. Prices and availability subject to change without notice.

To : Hodder & Stoughton Ltd, Cash Sales Department, Bookpoint, 39 Milton Park, Abingdon, OXON, OX14 4TD, UK. If you have a credit card you may order by telephone – 01235 831700.

Please enclose a cheque or postal order made payable to Bookpoint Ltd, allow the following for postage and packing: UK & BFPO: £1.00 for the first book, 50p for the second book and 30p for each additional book ordered up to a maximum charge of £3.00. OVERSEAS & EIRE: £2.00 for the first book, £1.00 for the second book and 50p for each additional book.

Please send me

	copies of 0 340 67418 0	Astral Projection	£5.99	£
	copies of 0 340 62082 X	Chakras	£5.99	£
	copies of 0 340 64804 X	Chinese Horoscopes	£5.99	£
	copies of 0 340 60882 X	Dowsing	£5.99	£
	copies of 0 340 60150 7	Dream Interpretation	£5.99	£
	copies of 0 340 62079 X	Feng Shui	£5.99	£
	copies of 0 340 60883 8	Gems & Crystals	£5.99	£
	copies of 0 340 60625 8	Graphology	£5.99	£
	copies of 0 340 67415 6	Herbs for Magic and Ritual	£4.99	£
	copies of 0 340 62080 3	I-Ching	£5.99	£
	copies of 0 340 64805 8	Love Signs	£5.99	£
	copies of 0 340 64835 X	Meditation	£5.99	£
	copies of 0 340 59551 5	Numerology	£5.99	£
	copies of 0 340 67013 4	Paganism	£5.99	£
	copies of 0 340 59552 3	Palmistry	£5.99	£
	copies of 0 340 67339 7	Qabalah	£5.99	£
	copies of 0 340 62081 1	Runes	£5.99	£
	copies of 0 340 67416 4	Spiritual Healing	£5.99	£
	copies of 0 340 59553 1	Star Signs	£5.99	£
	copies of 0 340 59550 7	Tarot	£5.99	£
	copies of 0 340 64836 8	The Moon and You	£5.99	£
	copies of 0 340 65495 3	Visualisation	£5.99	£
	copies of 0 340 67014 2	Witchcraft	£5.99	£
			TOTAL	£

Name ....

Address ....

....

.... Post Code ....

If you would prefer to pay by credit card, please complete:

Please debit my Visa/Access/Diner's Card/American Express (delete as appropriate) card no:

☐☐☐☐☐☐☐☐☐☐☐☐☐☐☐☐

Signature .... Expiry Date...

For sales in the following countries please contact:
UNITED STATES: Trafalgar Square (Vermont), Tel: 800 423 4525 (toll-free)
CANADA: General Publishing (Ontario), Tel: 445 3333
AUSTRALIA: Hodder & Stoughton (Sydney), Tel: 02 638 5299